# Enrollment Management

*An Integrated Approach*

Don Hossler

New York, College Entrance Examination Board, 1984

*To Carol-Anne*

Editorial inquiries concerning this book should be addressed to: Editorial Office, The College Board, 888 Seventh Avenue, New York, New York 10106.

Copies of this book may be ordered from College Board Publications, Box 866, New York, New York 10101. The price is $12.95.

ISBN: 0-87447-193-1.

Printed in the United States of America.

9 8 7 6 5 4 3 2 1

# Contents

*Figures*

## *Tables*

# *Preface*

The groundwork for this book has been laid over several years. As an administrator at California Lutheran College, I became intrigued with the college enrollment decision. At the time I was also a graduate student in higher education at Claremont Graduate School. In discussions with Howard Bowen, he suggested that the admissions field would be one of importance to colleges and universities in the coming years.

During conversations with admissions officers at California Lutheran, I was struck by the uncertainty that often surrounded their efforts. At times they were not sure how college nights, high school visits, and a variety of other activities actually influenced the college-choice process of prospective matriculants. I began to wonder if research in this area, as well as others, when applied to specific institutional settings, could enable colleges and universities to exert more control over their enrollments.

Small colleges offer a wealth of diverse experiences for students of higher education. In addition to my interest in college choice, I had the opportunity to work extensively in other areas related to the concept of enrollment management. Insights into the areas of student affairs, student attrition, and institutional planning were particularly valuable.

Moving from administration to a teaching position at Loyola University of Chicago enabled me to pursue these interests and to begin to integrate my experiences. Contact with graduate students and admissions officers in the Chicago area brought many ideas into focus. The interest and encouragement of the College Board provided the impetus to "get to work" on this book.

I have attempted to synthesize the literature on a number of topics related to the concept of enrollment management. The only areas consciously omitted from this work are nonprofit marketing and a review of recruitment tactics. Since this work is conceptual in nature, a section on recruitment tactics seemed too specific. As for nonprofit marketing, there are already a number of excellent sources on this topic.

The factors that influence college enrollments are varied and complex. Throughout this book I have attempted to extract the essence of research findings on issues ranging from the demand for higher education to the outcomes of higher education. The chapter on economic demand studies is the most technical. It is included because knowledgeable enrollment managers should understand some of the basic forces that impel large numbers of traditional and nontraditional learners to seek a college degree.

One need only scan the classified section of the *Chronicle of Higher Education* to see that the concept of enrollment management is rapidly gaining acceptance on college campuses. It is a developing field that will require more than an upgraded "admissions management" effort to be successful. Enrollment managers will need to be knowledgeable senior-level administrators in order to successfully organize enrollment management efforts. It is hoped that this work will help to lay the foundation for an emerging profession.

*Acknowledgments*

There are several people to whom I would like to give special thanks. My wife Carol-Anne, who has been a patient editor and an understanding companion as I spent many nights and weekends on this project. Our two children, David and Peter, who often asked when it was their turn to play with the computer, and when Dad would have more time to play with them. In addition I would like to thank Marian Claffey, my graduate assistant, and now the assistant to the dean of the Graduate School at Loyola. Because of her experience in admissions, her suggestions were always helpful as was her offer to review each chapter. Writing this book was a family affair: Shirley and Don Hossler and Barbara Hughes were closely involved in a final editing of the manuscript.

Terry Williams, my colleague and friend at Loyola, has put together an excellent chapter on student-institution fit, which has enhanced the scope of this book. His wife Pat did the typing and much of the editing on this section. Gloria Lewis, my department chairman, and Gerald Gutik, the dean of the School of Education, have offered support and assistance along the way.

Finally I would like to thank Jim Esmay for reviewing the chapter on economic demand as well as Jim Nelson, Sue Wetzel Gardner, and Joe Morsicato of the College Board. Jim Nelson's insightful comments and Sue's assistance were always timely and encouraging. Joe Morsicato's careful attention to the manuscript has been greatly appreciated.

Don Hossler

# Chapter 1

# Enrollment Management

## AN EMERGING PROFESSION

*Enrollment management . . . enrollment planning . . . optimizing enrollments.*
These terms reflect the dominant theme in the new agenda for the admissions profession. Maintaining enrollments has become a vital concern for
most institutions of higher learning in the United States. For the more
selective colleges and universities, the interest stems from a desire to
maintain a student body of high quality with an identifiable set of characteristics. Among less selective institutions, the efforts in enrollment management reflect a concern for attracting a sufficient number of students to
ensure health and vitality, to assure the significant survival of the institution.

The concern for collegiate enrollments is not a new phenomenon. The
history of United States higher education chronicles periods in the eigh-
teenth and nineteenth centuries when institutional vitality was threatened
by small enrollments (Brubacher and Rudy 1976; Rudolph 1962). In the
twentieth century the decade of the 1930s was also a period when institutions of higher learning, particularly private ones, experienced anxiety
over enrollments (Thresher 1966). Even the 1960s, generally regarded as
an era of massive growth for colleges and universities, was a time of
competition for students on some campuses. Doermann (1968) notes that
rising costs in the private sector, along with the rapid expansion of both
two- and four-year public institutions, created competition among some
private and public institutions. For the most part, however, during the last
forty-five years collegiate enrollments have been relatively stable or have
been growing. In most professions, professional memories extend only as
far as personal experiences. Thus, for most members of admissions staffs,
their professional lives have been ones of relative affluence in terms of
student enrollments.

The admissions field could trace its beginnings to Harvard's first official
statement on admissions criteria in 1642 (Broome 1963). Those who view
the specialty as a more active agent might point to some of the early

American college presidents who traveled the countryside seeking funds and students (Rudolph 1962). During the nineteenth century a slow but steady pattern of events began to shape admissions. Before 1870 colleges and universities relied upon their own individual admissions statements and individual entrance examinations (Broom 1963). In 1870, however, the University of Michigan began to certify, or accredit, state high schools and to guarantee admission to students graduating from these accredited high schools (Broome 1963). Colleges and universities across the country began to follow this pattern, but it did not promote consistency and uniformity in the college admissions process.

To address these concerns, a series of activities, beginning with a conference of New England colleges in 1879 and culminating in the report of the Committee on College Entrance Requirements, led to the creation of the College Entrance Examination Board in 1899 (Broome 1963). The emergence of the College Board, however, does not mark the beginning of the professional admissions function.

In the late 1920s and early 1930s, colleges and universities began to appoint the first administrative specialists who were to concern themselves with admitting students (Thresher 1966). Many of these new admissions specialists, unfortunately, never had the opportunity to address the issue of standards. The onset of the Great Depression brought with it pressures on college enrollments, and as a result many admissions professionals became recruiters as colleges attempted to increase their enrollments (Thresher 1966).

Following the Depression, the role of admissions personnel broadened. The emphasis on recruitment was greatly diminished. Instead, admissions officers were screening prospective applicants, examining credentials, and seeking students with the "right" characteristics for the institution. At many institutions this emphasis on admitting students led to a merging of the admissions and registrar offices because their functions were often similar. The creation of the American Association of Collegiate Registrars and Admissions Officers (AACRAO) reflects these historic ties. Even as late as the 1960s, the roles of admissions professionals and registrars were not clearly delineated (Hauser and Lazarsfeld 1964).

During most of the brief history of the profession, those responsible for maintaining enrollments at institutions of higher education operated from an admissions mode rather than a recruitment or marketing mode. Nevertheless, even at a time when admissions professionals were entering a period of unprecedented prosperity in terms of college applicants, societal and cultural forces were at work that would ultimately bring about the current dilemmas of the profession.

In 1944 the Servicemen's Readjustment Act (the GI Bill of Rights) was passed. In 1952 the benefits of the GI Bill were extended to the Korean War veterans under Public Law 552. This legislation had an important impact on colleges and universities by providing federal subsidies for returning GIs who wished to pursue a college education—and many did. These veterans did not look like the traditional students of the past. They attended public institutions for the most part and helped lead the demand for expanded programs at state colleges and universities. This demand signaled what has been described as the Golden Age of American higher education (Bowen 1977).

It was not simply the return of ex-servicemen that brought about this Golden Age. The nation entered an egalitarian period, which influenced every aspect of society. A high school diploma had become the universal standard of education and a college degree was rapidly becoming the "social escalator" to upward mobility (Jencks and Reisman 1968, p. 98). Working-class families began to urge their children to pursue higher learning and to support this pursuit in numbers larger than ever before (Andersen 1977). As a result many first-generation college students entered the system. In conjunction with this increased recognition of a college education, the arrival of the baby boom children further expanded the demand for higher education.

In addition to these demographic trends, changes in public policy occurred that also increased student demand. With the National Defense Education Act of 1958, followed by the Higher Education Act of 1965, the federal government began to take an active and direct role in encouraging attendance in and access to institutions of higher learning. The federal role accentuated the demand for a college education.

As the result of heightened federal support, the rising interest in higher education permitted some admissions officers to put aside their role of salesmen. The increasing numbers of students also made it possible for many elite colleges and universities to maintain their selection standards and enabled admissions professionals to continue to operate in an admissions mode. Nevertheless, the image of this group of administrators was not enhanced by these developments. Admissions personnel, in their brief history, have always suffered from a lack of respect within the academy (Hauser and Lazarsfeld 1964; Kemerer, Baldridge, and Green 1982). They have often seen themselves as second-class citizens. The lack of an identifiable body of knowledge requiring some expertise has caused many within colleges and universities to view admissions officers as less than professional. The oversupply of applicants suggested to faculty and collegiate administrators that the task of representing the college was relatively simple.

The arrival of the 1970s, however, marked the beginning of some significant changes for higher education in the United States. In 1966 Allen

Cartter began to predict a downturn in enrollments. Although his predictions went unnoticed for six years, by 1971 the U.S. Office of Education was projecting similar declines. The facts were simple. All the potential college matriculants could be counted and those numbers would level off and decline over the next 25 years (Cartter 1966). Institutions with less visibility and less student drawing power began to become concerned about future enrollments. It was rapidly becoming apparent to the higher education community that they were moving from a period of plenty to one of scarcity.

The coming demographic changes, nevertheless, were not the only factors influencing collegiate enrollments. In the first years of the 1970s the economic value of attending college, heretofore a civil religion of sorts, began to be questioned (Berg and Freedman 1977; Bird 1975; Hapgood 1971). College graduates were having greater difficulty finding jobs. Terms like underemployed and overqualified began to be used to describe college graduates. As this phenomenon continued, economists and social scientists began to suggest that fewer high school graduates would attend college (Dresch and Waldenberg 1978; Freeman and Hollomon 1975; Froomkin 1980). These predictions further heightened concerns over enrollments.

The rising costs of higher education produced by the inflationary cycles of the 1970s also aggravated worries about student enrollments. The costs continued to increase. Administrators, particularly those in the private sector, became concerned that many potential matriculants would no longer be able to afford a private college or university.

Most recently, public policy shifts at the state and federal levels have resulted in reduced allocations for direct subsidies and for aid to students. These developments seem to be the last straw in a litany of problems that place pressure on student enrollments as a source of tuition revenues.

Thus, the very changes that brought about the expansion of the colleges and universities between 1950 and 1970 have helped to create the current dilemmas. The higher education system expanded to meet a need for places during periods of high demand that will not be equaled until the late 1990s (McConnell and Kaufman 1984). The system grew so fast that it was prepared for an enrollment norm, which was in fact the peak of student enrollments. To some critics it appears that the egalitarianism of the last 25 years has resulted in a glut of college graduates. Finally, federal and state largesse has created a generation of potential matriculants who have become accustomed to financial aid assistance and may not be willing to pay for more of their own college education.

The changes that have occurred in the last 15 years have brought about many difficulties for the institutions and for the admissions personnel. Paradoxically, the value of admissions professionals has risen as rapidly as the problems of colleges and universities have increased. They may well be experiencing the greatest amount of visibility and respect they have ever had. Enrollment managers are reporting directly to college presidents on many campuses, sitting on senior administrative boards, and seeing the scope of their responsibilities redefined and expanded.

The admissions field is emerging as an area of crucial importance to many colleges and universities. Admissions professionals have opportunities to influence institutional policymaking at the highest level. To make contributions that are both insightful and recognized, many professionals must expand their knowledge of higher education in general and their expertise in enrollment management in particular. The study of enrollment management as a specific expertise holds the promise of establishing specialized knowledge for the admissions profession. This will be essential for enrollment managers as they seek to create an image within the academy that validates their elevated status, influence, and salary. An enhanced professional image based on specialized expertise, as well as success, will be of great value. Thus, a conceptual understanding of enrollment management is an important link to increased effectiveness and status.

## A WORKING DEFINITION

As the concern for student enrollment has increased, institutional leaders have come to realize that retaining matriculants is just as important as attracting them. The need to manage college enrollments from the point of initial student contact to the point of graduation has become increasingly apparent. As a result, the concept of enrollment management is quickly replacing the admissions model that focuses only on attracting and admitting qualified students. Enrollment management has generated a great deal of interest, yet it remains a new concept and one that is ill-defined.

Kemerer, Baldridge, and Green (1982) have described enrollment management as both a "concept" and a "procedure." As a concept they suggest that "enrollment management implies an assertive approach to ensuring the steady supply of qualified students required to maintain institutional vitality" (p. 21). In terms of a procedure they describe enrollment management as "a set of activities to help institutions to interact more successfully with their potential students" (p. 21). Managing enrollments includes all the traditional operations of an admissions office, but many other activities are involved as well.

Effective enrollment management not only requires the marketing of the institution and the selection of students but also involves more broadly based and all-encompassing activities. Enrollment management can be defined as a process, or an activity, that influences the size, the shape, and the characteristics of a student body by directing institutional efforts in marketing, recruitment, and admissions as well as pricing and financial aid. In addition, the process exerts a significant influence on academic advising, institutional research agenda, orientation, retention studies, and student services. It is not simply an administrative process. Enrollment management involves the entire campus.

Those accountable for enrollment management or planning must have direct responsibility for the following:

*1. Student Marketing and Recruitment.* Enrollment managers must have data that enable them to identify current and potential markets. They must communicate to inform, motivate, and service these markets. The ultimate goal is to recruit matriculants who will find attendance at the institution satisfying, stimulating, and growth-producing.

*2. Pricing and Financial Aid.* Since these two factors exert a significant influence on attendance, enrollment managers must have the authority (in consultation with other senior-level administrative officers) to set tuition levels and to award financial aid in such a way as to maximize student enrollment.

In addition to their direct responsibilities, enrollment managers need to be able to exert a strong influence on:

*3. Academic and Career Advising.* Advising has an important influence on the career decisions students make and is related to student satisfaction and persistence. An enrollment management plan must include these functions.

*4. Academic Assistance Programs.* Many current high school graduates are ill-prepared for college. Enrollment managers recruit and admit students and are, therefore, well acquainted with the strengths and weaknesses of these students. The office of enrollment management should inform the academic assistance center of the needs of incoming students. In return, the academic assistance center needs to advise the enrollment management office of the trends and the progress of students the center is assisting.

*5. Institutional Research.* The enrollment management office must have a high priority in the institutional research area. Data must regularly be gathered about the characteristics of potential and actual matriculants, student satisfaction, and student outcomes. Such information is essential for enrollment managers.

6. *Orientation.* Orientation programs prepare students for the environment they will be entering. Such programs can help reduce anxiety and facilitate students' success in their new environment. In some sense, orientation is the point at which the admissions office turns the entering class over to the institution. Orientation programs are viewed as an important part of any retention effort.

7. *Retention Programs.* This is the campuswide effort to improve student persistence. Sound retention efforts not only encompass good recruiting, advising, orientation programs, and research, but also involve faculty and staff in myriad ways that can improve retention. Typically, the responsibilities for retention are housed in the offices of academic affairs, enrollment services, or student services. Regardless of the office in which the responsibilities are located, the enrollment management office should be closely involved in retention efforts.

8. *Student Services.* Student services such as athletics, activities, career planning, counseling, and residence life have a major impact on the campus environment. Student services help shape the institution's attractiveness to potential students, as well as the ability of the college to keep matriculants. As a result, student services are an important part of an enrollment management plan.

The exact direct responsibilities of an enrollment planning office are not important. Enrollment managers, however, must be able to influence all these functions. This influence can occur by organizational mandate or simply via a sound working relationship among the individuals responsible for the above-mentioned areas. In either case, a successful enrollment management plan must include all these functions as part of an integrated effort.

Although enrollment management is a relatively new approach, a considerable body of research can be applied to this area. Some of the research, which is drawn from a variety of disciplines and fields of study, is readily accessible to college administrators, while other areas tend not to be widely known. As admissions officers make the transition from admissions and marketing modes to enrollment management, professional enrollment managers will increasingly draw upon this research foundation to inform their decisions.

## AN OVERVIEW

To plan for enrollments and to manage enrollments, professionals must begin with an understanding of the demand for higher education and of how students decide to enroll in a specific college or university. Demand studies enable enrollment planners to realize how the economy and the labor market affect enrollments. Are enrollments highly responsive to fluctuations in the economy and the labor market, or are noneconomic factors influential in the demand cycle? How do factors such as the rate of return, credentialism, and changes in the draft laws affect student demand for higher education? A review of the research will answer these questions. Readers will quickly discover, however, that like many of the social sciences, economics is not a precise science. Demand research provides an important background for understanding the aggregate demand for higher education. It enables enrollment planners to anticipate how changes in the economy might affect enrollments and leads naturally to college-choice research, which has greater direct usefulness for enrollment managers. Finally, an understanding of demand studies is an important step in the development of a specialized knowledge base for enrollment managers.

The literature on college choice is reasonably sophisticated and offers insight into the decision-making process of potential matriculants. Several models of the college-choice process help to identify the factors that influence the enrollment decision. Research on college choice assists enrollment managers to determine how they may be able to influence the choice process.

In addition to demand studies and college-choice research, pricing is a key element of the enrollment decision. Investigations on pricing provide a thorough understanding of how today's students are financing their college education. Research on pricing also reveals how changes in tuition affect enrollments and the relationship between financial aid and attendance. Also, a discussion of pricing would not be complete without a review of the role pricing plays in equity and in access to United States colleges and universities.

Enrollment management, however, is more than attracting matriculants. It also includes efforts to retain students once they arrive on campus. Perhaps the most important role that enrollment managers play is assisting students as they select the college that best meets their needs and interests. The notion of "fit" between the student and the institution is significant. Research in student-institution fit is useful background information for admissions professionals because there is a strong relationship between the "goodness" of fit and persistence. Effective professionals need to be able to assess the campus environment and identify potential students whose interests and characteristics are likely to be a good match with that environment. Environments can also be altered, and enrollment managers should be exposed to concepts of campus ecology and milieu management.

Along with the attempt to ensure a good match between student and campus, several other variables influence student persistence. Retention research and institutional retention programs have been widely written about in the last 10 years. It is necessary for professional enrollment managers to be familiar with these findings and to link student fit with retention activities.

Marketing, recruitment, and admissions activities, in addition to retention programs, are important responsibilities for enrollment planners and managers. These areas form the center of the specialized knowledge base, or expertise, of the emerging field of enrollment management. There is one other area of research, however, which is also a necessary foundation for professional administrators in this field: Enrollment managers should be well aware of the outcomes of higher education. Increasingly, admissions officers are being asked to articulate the benefits of higher education to students and parents, trustees, and at times to legislators and other elected officials. Professionals must be able to make a strong case for the institutions they represent. Outcomes research also provides the framework for the institutional research agenda essential for effective enrollment planning.

Outcomes research focuses primarily on two areas. First, the impact of college on students examines how students change during the college years and how college attendance affects student development. Some studies have looked at the specific changes from the freshman to the sophomore to the junior to the senior years. This can be particularly useful information for retention programs. Impact studies also document the moral, emotional, political, and intellectual development of students. These studies help to demonstrate that college does indeed make a difference!

Second, outcomes research examines the economic and noneconomic benefits that accrue to individuals and to society as a whole. In an era when both prospective students and society seem to be questioning the value of a college education, enrollment planners must be able to address the benefits question in an informed manner. An educated understanding of the outcomes of higher education can enhance the quality of written materials and presentations upon which enrollment officers depend.

Two themes evident throughout this book are the need for a new level of professionalism vis-à-vis a sound knowledge base and the need for a strong research and planning effort by enrollment managers. With the evolution of enrollment management, the admissions field has a specialized body of knowledge it can lay claim to and apply, demonstrating an enhanced level of expertise.

The need for planning cannot be minimized. Kemerer, Baldridge, and Green (1982) describe the importance of institutional research in enrollment planning as follows:

> Data collection is a critical yet often ignored component of enrollment management efforts. Most administrators do not have ready access to recruitment and retention data. Moreover, the organizational structure impedes the analysis and dissemination of data that are critical to informed policymaking (pp. 25–26).

Enrollment planners must be able to project enrollments, influence the college-choice process, determine an effective pricing structure, retain students, and measure outcomes. All of these activities rely heavily on planning and an adequate institutional data base. Professional enrollment managers have to be able to answer the following questions:

1. Why do students come to this institution?
2. What are the characteristics of the matriculants?
3. What are the salient characteristics of the campus environment?
4. What are the characteristics of the persisting students?
5. What are the characteristics of the dropouts?
6. How do students benefit from attending this institution?

Communication, marketing, and public relations skills will continue to be important but no longer sufficient for effective enrollment management. A knowledge base and research skills (or at least the ability to interpret data in meaningful ways) are essential for new professionals in this area.

A research foundation in enrollment management will provide this emerging profession with an expertise it can claim to be uniquely its own. An understanding of research done in areas linked to enrollment management provides a frame of reference. This reference frame, when combined with the new emphasis on nonprofit marketing (which is also based heavily on research and an adequate data base), will assist in setting long-range agenda for institutions and the admissions profession as well. Whether or not enrollments can actually be managed remains to be seen. I suspect that *influencing* enrollments may prove to be a much more accurate term. Unfortunately, enrollment influencing does not connote the same degree of competence and control as does enrollment managing. We shall return to this issue in the final chapter.

# PART ONE

The first part of this work looks at the primary determinants of college enrollment—the demand for higher education, the college-choice process, and the effects of tuition and financial aid on attendance. These topics are the cornerstone of a research foundation for enrollment managers.

In each chapter of Part One, findings that should shape the planning and marketing process of colleges and universities are examined. Some areas do not lend themselves as readily to control as do others. In total, however, they represent a wealth of information that provides a rationale for many activities that admissions personnel carry out instinctively. In addition, Chapters 2, 3, and 4 pose new questions and new approaches for enrollment managers.

# Chapter 2

# The Demand for Higher Education

## DEMAND AND CHOICE

Analysis of the demand for higher education has traditionally been the realm of economists. Because all levels of education require inputs of labor and capital, education is a form of economic activity. Thus, in their studies of education, economists have applied their discipline to the study of higher education. The demand for higher education is one aspect of these studies. Generally, demand research has been of little interest to the admissions profession. For emergent enrollment managers, however, demand literature offers a foundation for enrollment planning.

Demand studies focus on the aggregate student demand for places in colleges and universities and examine how economic and sociological factors influence that demand. Knowledge of this literature provides enrollment managers with a set of assumptions from which enrollment projections can be developed. Using demand studies, enrollment managers can more accurately project how recessions, upswings in the need for college-educated workers, and shifts in public policy can affect enrollments. In addition, this research is an important part of the specialized knowledge base that can professionalize and lend credibility to enrollment managers.

Before this discussion of the demand for higher education is continued, however, it is necessary to explain the distinctions between demand studies and college-choice research. Discussing studies on college choice separately from investigations into demand is somewhat arbitrary. Research on demand is broad in scope and includes trends in the economy, labor market activity, and other economic considerations as well as demographic, individual, and sociological variables. College-choice literature more specifically examines the college enrollment decision and looks at sociodemographic and individual student variables. In addition, however, these works often include demand factors such as socioeconomic status and rate of return. A research review such as this could readily treat both areas at the same time; for clarity and comprehension, they are discussed separately.

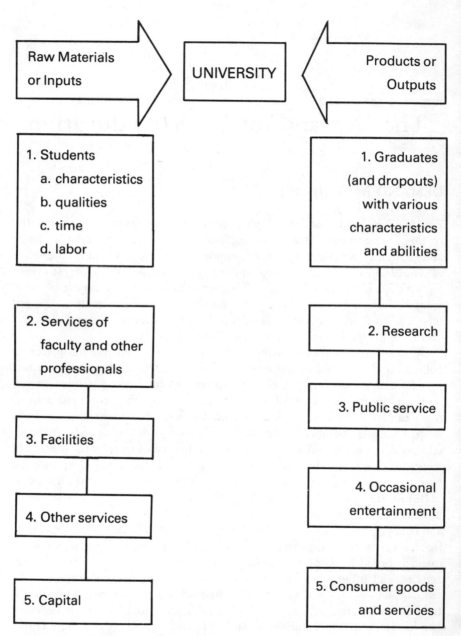

**Figure 1** The higher education industry.

Demand studies are covered in this chapter, and a review of the literature on college choice follows in Chapter 3.

A review of higher education as an industry, or economic activity, is essential to introduce some of the concepts and terminology that are part of the vernacular of economic studies. Following this section, quantitative demand formulas and theories are presented to provide a conceptual framework for understanding aggregate student demand for higher education. Finally, specific factors that influence demand are discussed. Although relatively little research has been conducted on demand at individual institutions, this chapter also explores research related to individual demand shifts from higher cost to lower cost institutions.

## HIGHER EDUCATION AS INDUSTRY

To review this literature, it is first necessary to look at colleges and universities in the same way economists do—as an industry, as shown in Figure 1.

The inputs—the time and labor of students, along with faculty, facilities, other services, and capital—are transformed over four years into the products of colleges and universities. These products include graduates, research, public service, and consumer goods and services.

This supply of student inputs corresponds to what is usually regarded as the demand for places by potential students (Radner and Miller 1975, p. 1). Thus, demand studies examine the relationships among the price of higher education, the employment opportunities for college graduates, the number of spaces colleges and universities have available for new matriculants, and the number of new students desiring to matriculate.

To make use of the studies, the reader must understand a number of terms commonly used in economics. These terms are defined below.

*Elasticity.* The measure of the degree of responsiveness of one variable ($y$) to changes in another variable ($x$). Thus, price elasticity of demand is the degree of change in demand for a quantity of a good based on changes in its price. The elasticity of $y$ with respect to changes in $x$ equals:

$$\frac{\text{proportional changes in } y}{\text{proportional changes in } x}$$

If the measure of elasticity is greater than 1, the good has an elastic demand; it is said to have unit elasticity if it is equal to 1. If it is less than 1, it is said to have inelastic demand. (See Figure 2.) In other words, if student

Elasticity of Student Demand for Higher Education

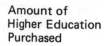

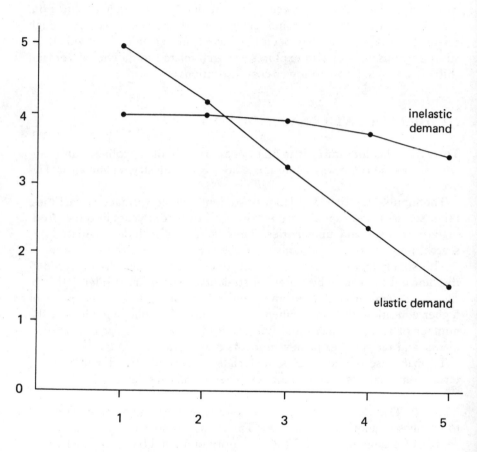

Price of
Higher Education

**Figure 2** Elasticity of student demand for higher education.

demand changes very little in the face of a 15 percent tuition increase, the demand for higher education at that institution can be described as inelastic. Elasticity, then, suggests price responsiveness on the part of the consumer; inelasticity suggests a lack of price responsiveness.

*Cross-Elasticity.* The likelihood that the consumer will substitute one product for another as the price differentials vary between two products. For instance, as the price of Harvard rises, there comes a point at which prospective students in Michigan will attend the University of Michigan instead of Harvard. Thus, the aggregate demand for higher education can be relatively inelastic; yet cross-elasticity can vary, which explains the variations in demand between high- and low-cost institutions.

*Economic, or Pecuniary, Benefits of Higher Education.* The individual financial benefits that accrue as the result of college attendance. These include such benefits as lifetime income, fringe benefits, employability, and job mobility.

*Noneconomic, or Psychic, Benefits of Higher Education.* The individual nonfinancial benefits that result from college attendance. These include such benefits as personal growth and development, happiness, improved use of leisure time, and improved health.

*Consumptive Benefits of Higher Education.* Those individual benefits enjoyed by students while attending college, such as going to sporting and cultural activities, making new friends, and having new experiences.

*Direct Costs.* The out-of-pocket costs of attending a college or university. These include tuition, books, travel expenses, and room and board.

*Opportunity Costs or Foregone Income.* The potential income that could have been earned by college students if they had been working full-time rather than attending a college or university.

*Rate of Return.* In this context, the income differential between college graduates and high school graduates. It can refer to the income differential during a given year, for a specified age cohort, or over a lifetime. The most meaningful statistic is the rate of return over a lifetime and is the context in which the term is used in this literature review.

*Credentialism.* The increasing tendency for employers to raise the entry-level educational requirements for careers. Credentialism has also been described as "diplomaism" and "sheepskin psychosis." Thus, the college

1. Enrollment ($E$) is a function ($f$) of costs ($C$)

$$(E) = f(C).$$

The proportion of the eligible population enrolling in colleges and universities depends on the direct costs and the opportunity costs of attendance.

2. The income level of potential students also affects demand ($I$)

$$(E) = f(C)(I).$$

3. Personal preference, motives, and aspirations also influence demand ($P$)

$$(E) = f(C)(I)(P).$$

4. The rate of return is yet another factor ($R$)

$$(E) = f(C)(I)(P)R.$$

**Figure** 3 Aggregate demand model.

$Q_i = f(Y_i, C_i, Z_i, P_i, R_i)$, where $i$ denotes any region of the country

$Q_i$ = number of high school graduates who wish to attend college in region $i$

$Y_i$ = expected rate of return in region $i$

$C_i$ = opportunity costs in region $i$

$Z_i$ = direct economic value of consumptive benefits in region $i$

$P_i$ = direct costs of attendance in region $i$

$R_i$ = discounted rate of return in region $i$ (because of inflation, current dollars are discounted over time)

Demand ($D_i$) thus is represented as follows:

$D_i = Q_i/N_i$, where $N_i$ is the eligible population in region $i$

**Figure** 4 Regional demand model.

degree becomes a screening device when, in fact, the job may not require the skills of a college degree holder.

## ANALYZING DEMAND: EMPIRICAL MODELS

The demand for places in institutions of higher learning is influenced by several factors: costs, income, student aspirations, projected benefits. These factors can be represented in the form of empirical models that express demand as a function of all of these components.

The equation in Figure 3 depicts aggregate demand on a national scale. This represents a rather simple model of demand. Figure 4 presents a more sophisticated demand model, which allows for regional variations. In both empirical models the key elements affecting demand are the following:

1. Direct costs
2. Opportunity costs
3. Number of potential matriculants in the population
4. Rate of return
5. Values, aspirations, and motivations of the potential matriculants

In attempts to quantify such demand equations, however, economists encounter some difficulties, for not all of the factors can be easily measured. One problem stems from attempts to quantify personal attitudes. How does one establish a numerical value for consumptive benefits like establishing lifelong friends or attending school social events? How can precise numbers be determined for the aspirations, values, and motivations of students? Determining the discounted rate of return can also be a problem. Some economists have attempted to determine discount rates on the basis of projected future inflation; others have tried to measure students' perceptions of discounted dollars and use these figures. In any case, enrollment managers should be aware that projecting demand is not a precise science. Economics, like many other disciplines, requires the use of assumptions that cannot always be determined with precision.

## ANALYZING DEMAND: DEMAND THEORIES

Another way to approach the demand for higher education is to examine demand theories as opposed to empirical models. Douglas Adkins, in his book *The Great American Degree Machine* (1975), outlines four basic demand theories. Three are based entirely on economic factors; the fourth

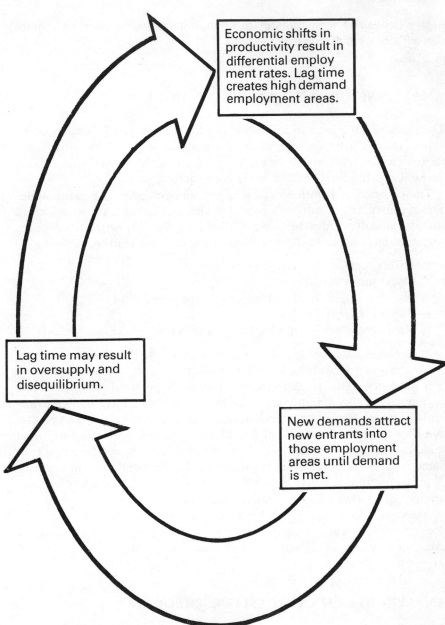

**Figure 5** Cobweb theorem of employment cycles.

is a sociological theory, which utilizes sociodemographic factors to explain demand.

## Economic Theories

Adkins's (1975) three economic demand theories—the technogenic, the disequilibrium, and the demand-inflation—seek to explain collegiate enrollments by monitoring shifts in productivity in the economy. These shifts, in turn, affect the pecuniary and nonpecuniary incentives offered by sectors in the labor market for college-trained manpower.

The technogenic model suggests that the magnitude, composition, and technology of economic activity are the principal external variables regulating the formation of college degree holders (p. 165). It assumes that potential matriculants respond to labor market inducements in their decision to pursue higher education and in their decision on which specialty, if any, to select. In the technogenic theory, employers may vary both the economic and the noneconomic benefits as inducements or disinducements to create optimum levels of college degree holders. The chain of causation is shown in Figure 5.

The second economic theory, the disequilibrium model, posits that the demand for college graduates will vary when (1) the human capital mechanism fails to bring the supply of college graduates and the demand for college graduates rapidly into line with one another or (2) the existing supply of college graduates is not absorbed into appropriate employment. Adkins states that the equilibrating forces are weak or operate over long lag times. As a result, economic activity in the labor market exerts a weak influence on potential matriculants. Thus, the assumption is that there is no well-defined mechanism of communication between the labor market and potential degree holders. Adkins further postulates that the total demand for higher education could be explained by the disequilibrium model, but that the technogenic model should still be used to explain students' choice of specialty or major.

Finally, the demand-inflation theory, like the technogenic theory, assumes that potential degree holders are responsive to labor market inducements. Unlike the technogenic model, however, this theory takes into consideration the labor market forces "that are likely to produce a smoothly increasing demand for degree holders that is largely unrelated to production or any other significant social forces. Hence the term inflation" (Adkins, p. 169). Thurow (1974), as an example, suggests that employers will use education as a way to minimize search and training costs. This enables employers to take fewer risks in hiring and inflates the need for college graduates. Excesses of college degree holders can still occur in this model.

If labor market inducements are not responded to, the result will be underemployment, or even unemployment.

## A Sociological Theory

In contrast to the three economic theories discussed above, which focus on activity in the labor market, Adkins also puts forth a sociological model that relies exclusively on noneconomic factors to explain the demand for higher education. His sociogenic theory simply asserts that historical and socioeconomic forces have impelled greater proportions of each successive age cohort to pursue a college education (p. 167). Retirement, birth rates, and death rates have been recognized as the principal forces affecting college enrollment rates. These variables are seen to affect enrollment rates in a relatively consistent manner.

Each of the four models presented here has strengths and weaknesses. The technogenic model, for instance, would predict declining enrollments in periods of declining rates of return, while the three other models might predict increased demand for a college education. The efficacy of these four theoretical approaches, however, is not the primary purpose of this chapter. The four demand theories assist in understanding collegiate enrollment patterns and also establish a backdrop against which some specific factors that influence demand can be explored. Nevertheless, at the end of this chapter, after such variables as employment rates and the rate of return are reviewed, these demand models will be reexamined briefly for evaluation.

## FACTORS THAT AFFECT DEMAND

The demand for higher education is influenced by a number of factors. Those that can affect enrollment include economic activity and resulting employment levels, rate of return, changes in the armed forces and draft legislation, pricing policies, and demographic changes. Because an entire chapter (Chapter 4) is devoted to the effects of net price and financial aid on attendance, these areas are omitted from this section. Research that indicates how the other factors affect demand will now be examined.

### Economic Activity

If student demand for higher education is stimulated by economic activity and the subsequent needs of the labor market, it should be possible to look at past economic boom-and-bust periods to see their impact on college enrollments. A relationship between the labor market and student demand suggests that enrollments should drop during periods of depression or recession and rise in years of high economic activity.

For instance, during the Great Depression a decline in student demand for higher education could certainly have been anticipated. Surprisingly, though, there was no decline in college attendance. During the decade of the 1930s baccalaureate degree holders actually increased by 79 percent over the previous decade (Adkins 1975, p. 172). In addition, the percentage of students seeking advanced degrees increased each year between 1930 and 1940 by at least 2.4 percent (p. 172).

The 1950s and 1960s were generally a period of steady economic growth. As might be expected, college enrollments increased. Between 1950 and 1969 college enrollments increased by over 4 million students, an almost threefold increase (Andersen 1977, p. 75.61).

During the 1970s there was a decreased demand for college-educated manpower. Although there was a leveling off from past rates of enrollment expansion, college enrollments actually continued to increase. Reduced opportunities for college graduates did not result in reduced student demand, as might have been anticipated.

From 1980 to 1983 further declines in the economy took place. Unemployment reached post-Depression highs. Despite this, college enrollments did not experience large declines. In 1980 and 1981 enrollments actually increased slightly (*Chronicle of Higher Education,* Nov. 4, 1981, p. 1). In 1982 enrollments decreased almost imperceptibly by 0.1 percent (*Chronicle of Higher Education,* Nov. 24, 1982, p. 1). This decrease is generally attributed to the long anticipated downturn resulting from fewer numbers of high school graduates—the traditional college matriculants. In an analysis of these enrollment trends vis-à-vis labor market activity, the complexity of these economic periods must be taken into consideration. During depressionary or recessionary cycles, when jobs are scarce, the opportunity costs of college attendance decrease. At such times students may often opt for higher education as an alternative to unemployment (Corrazzini, Dugan, and Grabowski 1972).

## Rate of Return

If student demand is influenced by economic considerations, fluctuations in the rate of return should also affect collegiate enrollments. In the 1950s Becker (1964) estimated that the individual rate of return on a college education over a lifetime was 14.5 percent for white males (p. 126). T. W. Schultz (1963) concluded that the average college graduate earned $120,000 more than did the average high school graduate over a lifetime (p. 72).

In the past 15 years the rate of return has received closer scrutiny. Earlier rate-of-return studies did not control for such variables as ability, socio-economic status, intergenerational effects of education, and sex. In addition, some of these earlier studies might not be valid for an era in which the supply of college graduates may exceed the demand. In the 1970s several studies emerged that did consider these variables (Douglas 1977; Freeman 1975; Juster 1975; Taubman and Wales 1973). This new research reports rates of return ranging from 4 to 11 percent. The most recent works in this area suggest that the rate of return on a college education has remained relatively stable since the mid-1970s (Freeman 1980; Mattila 1982).

Dresch, among others, has suggested that declines in the rate of return should have a negative influence on student demand. Dresch and Waldenberg (1978) state that a decline of $7,500 in the lifetime rate of return for men would result in a 6 to 13 percent decline in their rates of enrollment (p. 1). Among women, a similar decline would produce a 15 to 24 percent reduction in enrollments (p. 1). Research conducted by Mattila (1982) also concludes that severe declines in the rate of return have resulted in correspondingly large declines in enrollment rates among young males. The work of Dresch and Waldenberg and Mattila, however, seems to contradict other findings that imply the rate of return is not so important as other factors in determining enrollment patterns. According to Campbell and Siegel (1967) and Bishop (1977), the rate of return has an effect on demand, but it is not nearly so important as factors such as tuition costs and disposable family income. Bishop concludes that the rate of return either is not considered with any accuracy or is discounted at very high rates (p. 301). Campbell and Siegel and Bishop all conclude that the rate of return does not play a significant role in expanding or decreasing enrollment rates.

In total, it would seem that aggregate enrollment figures lend more support to the statement that fluctuations in the rate of return do not greatly affect collegiate enrollments. It must be noted, however, that aggregate figures mask shifts among various subgroups within the total numbers of matriculants. Between 1969 and the mid-1970s the number of young men of college age did decline by approximately 19 percent (Mattila, p. 250). This decrease was offset, however, by increases in the number of young women and older adult students entering colleges and universities.

## Credentialism

Many critics have suggested that credentialism is forcing Americans to pursue a product (higher education) that is declining in value. Nevertheless, unlike the labor market or the rate of return, credentialism is one of the factors identified as maintaining student demand for higher learning. Regardless of the criticisms of the inflationary process of diplomaism, the upgrading of educational requirements has made the college degree a necessity for employment.

Increasingly there are fewer and fewer uncredentialized industries left. In the past two decades the list of occupations in many regions for which a college diploma has become a prerequisite includes the following:

1. Allied health fields
2. Broadcasting
3. Early childhood education
4. Hotel and restaurant management
5. Insurance fields
6. Law enforcement
7. Many areas of sales
8. Recreation

Credentialism is not only being fostered by employers, but is encouraged by students and consumers of education. As Rawlins and Ulman (1975) point out, employers through professional organizations constantly push to upgrade the educational requirements of their professions (p. 232). Students increasingly use education as a hedge against unemployment or low-status employment.

The facts still indicate that higher education exerts a positive influence on employability. Bowen, in *Investment in Learning* (1977) states that for both men and women, unemployment varies inversely with the level of education (p. 167). Currently, among young adults, the unemployment rate for non–college graduates is almost three times that of college graduates; among blacks the gap is even larger (Young 1980, p. 40). The evidence indicates that credentialism has a positive influence on student demand.

## Armed Forces

Thus far, only economic factors have been examined in this review of the demand for places in colleges and universities. In addition to the previously discussed market activities, nonmarket factors, such as changes in public policy as it relates to the armed services, can have an effect on college enrollments. When the armed services are expanding, they can absorb high school graduates who might otherwise go directly into college (Galper and Dunn 1969). In addition, large numbers of veterans being discharged can also increase enrollments. Almost 50 percent of all new matriculants between 1946 and 1949 were World War II veterans financed by the GI Bill (Galper and Dunn, p. 765). Galper and Dunn conclude, however, that rapid expansion of the armed forces has greater potential for reducing

enrollments than large numbers of discharges have for expanding enrollments (pp. 775–776).

## Demographic Trends

Perhaps the most potent nonmarket stimulus to student demand is simply
the number of potential matriculants. Every enrollment manager is aware
that the number of potential traditional-age college students will decline
nationally during the 1980s and 1990s (McConnell and Kaufman 1984, p.
10). In the Northeast enrollments are projected to decline by as much as
18 percent by 1987 and by 35 percent by 1994; even by 1999 enrollments
will still experience a 30 percent reduction (p. 10). In the North Central
states, declines are expected to hit lows of 19 percent in 1986 and 29
percent in 1994 (p. 10). Although the nontraditional student has been
touted as a potential source of replacement for the decreasing numbers of
traditional students, this is doubtful. As Frances (1980) points out, since
three part-time students are the equivalent of one full-time student, they
cannot be expected to offset totally the reduced numbers of high school
graduates (p. 12).

## INDIVIDUAL DEMAND AND CROSS-ELASTICITY

As previously mentioned, little research has been conducted on the demand
for higher education at individual institutions. Similarly, there have been
very few investigations on cross-elasticity, or the substitution of one form
or type of higher education for another—for example, substituting low-
cost for high-cost or more prestigious for less prestigious institutions.

   In a study conducted by Ghali, Miklius, and Wada (1977), the authors
examined price-induced cross-elasticities between competing public and
private colleges and between two-year and four-year colleges.

   They assert that the cross-elasticities between various types of institutions are really quite small. According to the authors, high school graduates
select the educational alternative that has the greatest utility for them. The
implications of this research are that there is actually little competition
between the various sectors of the higher education community. Since this
study was conducted in the Hawaiian Islands, a unique geographical setting,
the results can by no means be viewed as conclusive. Although other studies
suggest some application overlap among the various sectors (Litten, Sullivan, and Brodigan 1983; Maguire and Lay 1980; Zemsky and Oedel 1983),
it appears that substitution between high-cost private and low-cost public
alternatives is not pronounced.

   Most of this research, however, was conducted before the shifts in public policy at the federal level. Recent reductions in financial aid, which might be characterized as a shift back from choice to access, may well be affecting enrollment patterns. These reductions in financial aid may not be reducing the aggregate demand, but they could be producing a substitution of low-cost colleges for high-cost colleges. In 1982 enrollments in private bachelor-degree-granting institutions fell by 1.5 percent and rose by 0.3 percent at public four-year colleges (*Chronicle of Higher Education,* Nov. 24, 1982, p. 7). In 1972, 766 students out of every 1,000 were enrolled in public colleges and universities; by 1982, this figure had jumped to 783 (p. 7)! It is possible that declining federal aid is resulting in more students opting for lower cost public alternatives.

Cross-elasticity can also be the result of perceptions of institutional prestige. An increasing body of evidence indicates that many students, if given the opportunity, will choose more selective and prestigious colleges and universities (Rowse and Wing 1982; Willingham and Breland 1982). In an era when the pool of traditional applicants is declining, the more selective schools may go deeper into their applicant pool, accepting students who might not otherwise have been accepted or have been offered financial assistance. The implications of these findings are that less prestigious institutions, both private and public, might experience enrollment declines greater than projected overall decreases.

## SUMMARIZING THE INFLUENCES ON DEMAND

Several theories and models have been analyzed in this chapter to describe the demand for higher education. Based on the discussions of labor market activity and the rate of return, neither the technogenic theory nor the disequilibrium theory appears to explain adequately the demand for higher education. Either the sociogenic model or the demand-inflation model seems to explain more accurately the steadily increasing, and more recently stable, enrollment patterns. As Adkins (1975) suggests, however, the technogenic model may still explain student selection of majors. Although a variety of factors affect student demand for places at colleges and universities, some factors appear to exert more influence than do others. Public policy shifts in areas like the armed services and financial aid, along with credentialism and demographic trends, have the strongest influences on demand.

Some of the more recent trends affecting enrollments, such as the reduction in federal funds for higher education (combined with a recession) and the declining numbers of high school graduates, may have a significant impact. These developments, if historical trends are maintained, may not affect the aggregate demand, but they may affect cross-elasticities, thus influencing enrollment patterns within the various sectors of the higher education system in the United States.

For enrollment managers, demand literature provides a background for enrollment planning. With the recent emphasis on strategic and long-range planning, enrollment managers are often asked to project enrollments over the next three to five years. Understanding the elements that affect student demand can be an important part of the environmental analysis advocated in strategic planning (Kotler and Murphy 1981).

Unfortunately, demand research cannot answer specific questions about the way various factors can influence student demand at an individual institution. It can, nevertheless, provide some guidelines and assist enrollment managers in making assumptions as a part of their planning:

1. The aggregate student demand for higher education is relatively unresponsive to the following:
   a. Increases and decreases in labor market activity
   b. The demand for college-trained manpower
   c. The rate of return
2. Demographic trends and credentialism appear to be largely responsible for determining the aggregate demand for higher education.
3. Public policy shifts, particularly in the areas of legislation affecting the armed forces and student financial assistance, can influence aggregate student demand.
4. The effects of an apparent retreat on the part of the federal government from efforts to eliminate financial barriers to higher education should be monitored carefully by enrollment managers. These developments may affect cross-elasticities among institutions, adversely affecting enrollments in the private sector.
5. Enrollment managers should closely monitor any shifts in enrollment from less prestigious to more prestigious colleges and universities (both public and private). A declining pool of traditional-age college students may adversely affect student demand at less prestigious schools. This could place the more expensive, less selective private colleges in an extremely vulnerable position.

Although research is not yet able to explain all aspects of students demand, it does provide a research foundation for enrollment management. It enables managers to better anticipate shifts in demand patterns. A conceptual understanding of the demand for higher education is a part of the expertise of enrollment management.

## SUGGESTIONS FOR FURTHER READING

For those interested in a more thorough and complete discussion of the demand for higher education and the other issues that have been presented, I recommend the following sources. Full particulars of publication are given in the Bibliography.

*The Great American Degree Machine,* by Douglas Adkins.
"The Labor Market and Higher Education," by Margaret Gordon and Carol Ahladeff. In the Carnegie Council on Policy Studies in Higher Education, *Three Thousand Futures: The Next Twenty Years for Higher Education.*
*Diplomaism,* by David Hapgood.
*The Outlook for Higher Education,* by Carol Frances.
*Demand and Supply in U.S. Higher Education,* by Roy Radner and Leonard Miller.
"Forecasting Economic and Demographic Conditions," by Paul Wing. In Paul Jedamus, Marvin Peterson, and Associates (eds.), *Improving Academic Management: A Handbook of Planning and Institutional Research.*

*Chapter 3*

# College Choice

## THE ENROLLMENT DECISION—AN OVERVIEW

The enrollment decision—choosing a college—has been widely studied by sociologists, psychologists, and educational researchers. The college-choice process is a complex phenomenon, a product of the background characteristics of students—their abilities, aspirations, and motivations—the attitudes and plans of close friends and family, as well as the characteristics and activities of the institutions of higher learning that fall within the students' choice sets. Chapter 2 examined the demand for higher education and how demand affects college enrollments. In this chapter the college-choice process is reviewed to determine how students go about selecting a college or university. First there is an overview of the enrollment decision and the factors that influence it. Then college choice is broken down into two major areas: (1) student characteristics and how those variables affect the choice process and (2) institutional characteristics and the effect these have on the enrollment decision.

An analysis of the enrollment decision will enable enrollment managers to understand the choice process and, as a result, lead to more effective strategies for influencing enrollments. D. Chapman (1981) writes:

> With increasingly intense competition for students, many colleges have persisted in the belief that they can affect students' choice merely by modifying their institutional descriptions or targeting their recruiting. Few admissions officers operate from a systematic model; colleges may overlook ways to increase the effectiveness of their recruiting, or conversely, overestimate the influence of the recruiting activities in which they do engage (p. 482).

The ability to manage enrollments is closely tied to a thorough understanding of college choice. For potential matriculants, the decision to attend a college or university is multidimensional.

Background characteristics such as parental education and financial and socioeconomic levels strongly correlate with participation rates in higher education. In addition to the socioeconomic status of the student and his

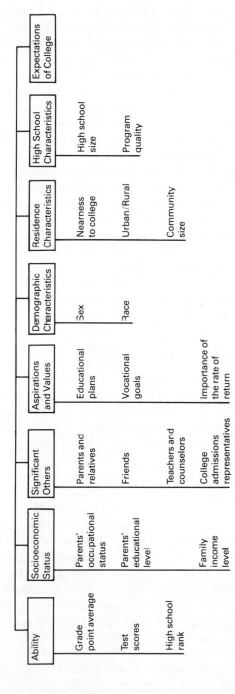

**Figure 6** Personological variables in the enrollment decision.

or her family, the ability level and the academic achievement pattern of the student, as well as the high school curriculum the student is enrolled in, are closely tied to attendance. Historically, the sex and race of potential students have also been related to the likelihood of attendance (these factors, however, appear to be diminishing in importance). The attitudes of high school seniors toward education in general and higher education specifically, in conjunction with their future aspirations, are also important in the choice of a college. Finally, in addition to all the other variables, significant others and residence characteristics influence the enrollment decision. These factors in total might be considered the personal variables in the enrollment decision—that is, the variables associated with the characteristics of potential matriculants that can influence their enrollment decisions. The personal elements of the decision to enroll are presented in Figure 6.

These individual variables are not the only elements, however, that influence the enrollment decision. There are also the characteristics of colleges and universities. As seen in Figure 7, institutional characteristics can be described as fixed and fluid. The fixed characteristics include such dimensions as location and sponsorship. Fluid characteristics include such factors as pricing policies, institutional programs, and methods of communication.

Gregory Jackson (1982) has presented a model of the college-choice process in which he describes the stages students move through in selecting the institutions they will attend (Figure 8).

In Jackson's model the first phase is most heavily influenced by individual variables such as those described in Figure 6. Jackson suggests that academic achievement, significant others (social context), and family background are the most influential factors in phase 1. During phase 2 students begin to weigh their preferences against the types of institutions they believe they can consider. At this point the characteristics of the colleges the student is considering begin to interact with the student preferences. Jackson reports that the most influential variables during this stage are geography, followed by information about the institutions. By the time the student arrives at phase 3, the most important decisions have been made. A broad list of potential colleges and universities has been narrowed to a small "choice set" (p. 239). At this stage institutional characteristics such as the net cost, academic programs, and other environmental characteristics become the deciding factors in the college-choice decision. Thus, the enrollment decision is interactional, depending on both the attributes of the student and the characteristics of the institutions the student perceives to be in his or her choice set. The student attributes and the institutional characteristics will now be examined in greater detail.

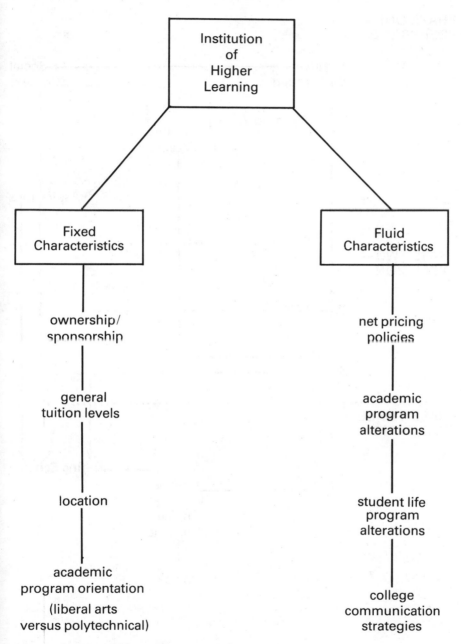

**Figure 7** Institutional variables in the enrollment decision.

**PHASE ONE—
PREFERENCE**

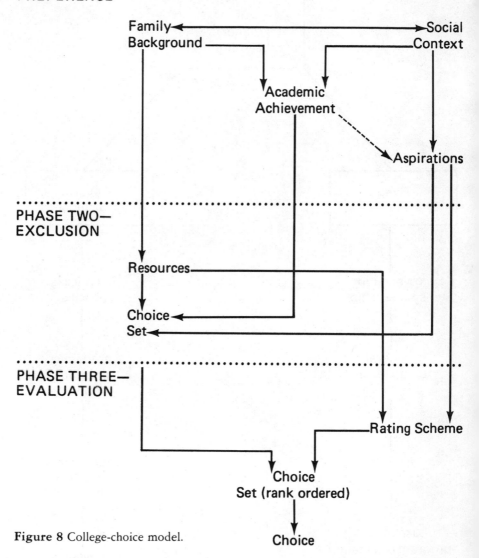

**Figure 8** College-choice model.

## PERSONOLOGICAL VARIABLES

### Ability and Achievement

The importance of ability and achievement in the enrollment decision is clearly evident. In *Talent and Society* (1958), McClelland et al. are careful to point out that performance (achievement) is not the same as potential (ability). McClelland goes on to state, however, that achievement in school is usually a good indicator of ability. The two terms are used alternately in this section because some research has focused on attempts to measure the relationship between student ability and college attendance. Other efforts have looked at the correlation between actual achievement and enrollment. In either case the results have been similar.

Ability helps to determine whether or not a student will want to go to college. Achievement also influences what kind of college or university a student aspires to attend and whether or not the applicant will be admitted. Student ability plays an important role in the college enrollment decision.

Grade point average, class standing, and IQ scores have been found to be positively related to college attendance. Tillery (1973) reports that 80 percent of those high school students who described themselves as having excellent grades planned to enroll in college (pp. 93 94). In contrast, 77 percent of those reporting that they had poor grades did not plan to attend a college or university. Research on the relationship between class standing and college attendance suggests that as many as 70 percent of students in the top half of their graduating class attend college as compared with approximately 40 percent of those in the bottom quartile (Daughtry 1960; Little 1960; State University of New York 1969).

Hause (1969) describes an average IQ differential of 13 points between high school graduates and college graduates (p. 131). According to Peters (1977), high-ability students are eight times more likely to go to college than are low-ability students (p. 9). Mare (1980) and Rumberger (1982) also conclude that ability is an important determinant of college-going behavior.

### Socioeconomic Status

The student's ability and socioeconomic status (SES) are probably the most influential variables in the college enrollment decision (Kohn, Manski, and Mundel 1972; Bishop 1977; Miller 1976). Trent and Medsker (1968) state "There is some question as to whether socioeconomic status or academic aptitude has the greater influence on the decision to attend college" (p. 3). The recent works of both Litten, Sullivan, and Brodigan (1983) and Zemsky and Oedel (1983) suggest that the combination of ability and socio-economic status influences the level of sophistication of the choice process. Corrazini, Dugan, and Grabowski (1972) conclude that SES has a cumulative effect throughout preschooling and the formal years of schooling. Solmon and Taubman (1973) report that 78 percent of students from the upper and upper middle class go to college, while only 15 percent of the lower class go to college (p. 326). In his research on college attendance, Peters (1977) notes that high SES students are four times more likely to go to college than are low SES students (p. 9). Numerous researchers have come to the same conclusion: a strong positive correlation exists between socioeconomic status and college attendance (Mare 1980; Perlman 1973; Trent and Medsker 1968; Whithey 1971).

## Significant Others

As Figure 6 indicates, other people who are close to high school students can play a role in the college enrollment decision. Parents, other family members, friends, teachers, counselors, and admissions counselors can influence the decision-making process of high school students. These are the "significant others" of the enrollment decision.

Parents exercise the greatest influence in the decision to go to college (Harnqvist 1978). Soper (1971) reports that Utah high school seniors list their parents as the most influential persons in shaping their post–high school plans (p. 32). Litten, Sullivan, and Brodigan (1983) found a good deal of similarity in the reasons matriculants and their parents gave for selecting one institution over another. Conklin and Dailey (1981) conclude that consistent parental encouragement is positively associated with college entry. In fact, their data suggest that the degree of consistency in parental encouragement helps to determine the likelihood of a student's entering a four-year college, a two-year college, or no college. As the consistency in parental encouragement for going to college declines, so does the likelihood of attending any college (Conklin and Dailey 1981). Other work by Trent and Medsker (1968) and Tillery (1973) indicates that students planning to enroll in a college are almost twice as likely to report that their parents expected them to enroll.

Here again we see the interrelatedness of these variables. Sewell and Shah (1978) state that SES, IQ, and parental encouragement account for 37 percent of the variance in college attendance plans (p. 12). Note that the mother's level of education is more highly correlated with the enrollment decision than is the father's level of education (Harnqvist 1978).

In addition to parents, others can play a role in the college-choice process. Investigations into factors that influence college-going behavior indicate that friends can be almost as important as parents (Coleman 1966; Distribution of High School Graduates and College Going Rates—New York State 1974; Tillery 1973). Although parents and friends are the most important significant others, teachers and high school counselors can also affect the plans of high school students (Tillery 1973). Of particular interest to enrollment managers are studies concluding that college admissions counselors are usually rated last in terms of their effect on student enrollment plans (Russell 1980; Tillery 1973). This raises hard questions regarding the role of the typical admissions counselor, which will be addressed at the end of this chapter.

## Student Aspirations and Values

The personological variables that influence the college enrollment decision are often linked in some way. The relationship between SES and ability has already been discussed. The aspirations of students have an important impact on the decision to go to college. Student aspirations, however, are also closely connected with their socioeconomic status and their ability (Tillery and Kildegaard 1973; Corrazini, Dugan, and Grabowski 1972). Thus, although Figure 6 presents most of these factors as independent variables, it must be remembered that they interact.

Their aspirations and career plans exert a strong influence on the postsecondary education plans of high school students. The obvious is often overlooked in sociological research. One of the best predictors of college attendance is the stated plan of a high school senior. Students who rate education an important value are more likely to attend college (Trent and Medsker 1968; Yankelovich 1972). Peters (1977, p. 11) reports:

- 81.5 percent of those planning to enter a four-year college actually enrolled
- 63 percent of those planning to enter a two-year college actually enrolled
- 9.6 percent of those planning to attend a two-year college actually ended up in a four-year institution
- 7.3 percent of those planning to enter a four-year college actually went to a two-year college

Hilton (1982), in an analysis of the National Longitudinal Study of 1972, also finds that most students follow through on their post–high school plans. He notes that almost 87 percent of those who did not plan at all to go on to college in fact did not (p. 5). In addition, several studies indicate that students who have decided upon a specific career or vocational objective are more likely to enroll (Beezer and Hjelm 1961; McQuitty and Tully 1970; Tillery and Kildegaard 1973).

Chapter 2 examined the demand for higher education. One of the economic factors analyzed was the relationship between the rate of return and college enrollment. Another attitudinal variable is the relative importance that students ascribe to higher education as a means to a higher income. As previously mentioned, the works of Bishop (1977) and Campbell and Siegel (1967) seem generally to suggest either that students are not greatly influenced by the rate of return or that they discount the rate of return at high levels. Nevertheless, other research indicates that the rate of return can influence the enrollment plans of some students (Dresch and Waldenberg 1978; Hossler 1979; Mattila 1982).

## Demographic Characteristics

Historically, the sex and race of students have had a significant impact on collegiate enrollments. In the past, women and minorities attended college in much smaller numbers than did white males. During the last two decades, however, the nation has made large strides in the educational opportunities available to women and minorities. As recently as 1974, there was a 5 percent difference in the attendance rates of men and women (School Enrollment—Social and Economic Characteristics of Students 1974, p. 1). Since that time, changes in social attitudes and public policy have resulted in a large increase in the enrollment rates for women. Currently, slightly more women than men are enrolled in United States colleges and universities.

The enrollment rates for black students have also tended to be less than those of white males. Since the civil rights movement of the 1960s, however, the participation rates of black students in higher education have been increasing steadily. Between 1966 and 1977 the number of black students enrolled in institutions of higher education tripled (*Chronicle of Higher Education,* June 1978, p. 8). In this same period the number of white students increased by only 51 percent (p. 18). Such data suggest that the enrollment gap has indeed been narrowed. Recent surveys point out that the attendance rates of black and white students are 37 percent and 40 percent respectively (Rumberger 1982, p. 462).

Hispanic students have also historically attended colleges and universities in smaller numbers. Again, recent statistics indicate that the situation is changing. Rumberger notes that the participation rates among Hispanic high school students is now 40 percent (p. 462). It must be remembered, nevertheless, that a high proportion of Hispanic high school students do not graduate from high school (Breneman 1983, p. 15). This clearly diminishes the total number of Hispanic students eligible for higher education.

## Residence Characteristics

Where students live also influences the college enrollment decision. After examining the relationship between college enrollments and residence characteristics, Willingham concludes that "proximity has become a key element in the accessibility of higher education" (1970, p. 9). Anderson, Bowman, and Tinto (1972) and Harnqvist (1978) note that proximity to an institution of higher learning is the most important dimension of students' residence characteristics. Students who live within a 20-mile radius of a college are more likely to attend a college or university (Anderson, Bowman, and Tinto 1972, p. 9). Although proximity to a college or university can influence attendance, it does not play as important a role as such factors as ability, SES, or peers.

Along with proximity, factors such as community size can also affect enrollment patterns. Anderson and colleagues note that students from large communities as well as urban settings (compared with rural settings) have higher enrollment rates. Here also it is important to note that these variables are not independent of other variables. There is a positive correlation among proximity to colleges, community characteristics, and socioeconomic status.

Residence status increasingly plays another kind of role in the college enrollment decision. More and more, students are demonstrating an unwillingness to travel out of their home state to attend an institution of higher education. Demographic studies (Linney 1979, p. 3; Peterson and Smith 1979, p. 1) document a steady increase in the number of students deciding to remain in their home state to pursue higher education:

1958—81 percent
1963—81 percent
1968—83 percent
1975—85 percent
1979—87 percent

Approximately 90 percent of all students enrolled in public colleges and universities are attending institutions in their home state (Peterson and Smith, p. 5). This compares with 67 percent at private institutions. Some of the states with the highest percentages of student out-of-state migration include Connecticut 70 percent; Nevada 72 percent; New Hampshire 66 percent; New Jersey 71 percent; New Mexico 73 percent; and Vermont 72 percent (p. 4). Peterson and Smith conclude that all data suggest the mobility of students will continue to decline.

## High School Characteristics

High school characteristics also may be included within the general heading of personal variables. It is no surprise that students enrolled in college preparatory courses are more likely to attend an institution of higher education (Peters 1977). Kolstad (1979) arrives at a similar conclusion, but cautions that the type of high school program is only weakly correlated with college attendance. Harnqvist (1978) finds that high school curriculums with greater amounts of science and mathematics are related to later college matriculation. Alexander et al. (1978) note a strong relationship between the quality, or status, of the school and college attendance. In addition, students who participate in extracurricular activities are more likely to enter a college or university.

In addition to these dimensions of quality, high school size is related to college enrollment. Students from larger high schools are more likely to attend a college or university than are students from small high schools (Anderson, Bowman, and Tinto 1972, p. 286). Although none of these variables has the predictive strength of factors like SES, ability, or parental influence, they are positively related to college attendance.

## General Expectations of College

The expectations students have of a college—what they expect it to look like, the kind of environment they anticipate—do affect their decision making. Unfortunately, the evidence suggests that most students do not have a clear notion of what to expect from a university and therefore may make poorly informed decisions. Litten, Sullivan, and Brodigan (1983) caution against assuming too much rationality in the college-choice decision of traditional-age college students. Jackson (1980) states that students often exclude institutions from their choice set that should be included. Similarly, Stern (1965) notes that students base decisions on stereotypes, that accurate information is often ignored or distorted, and that many students enter college with unrealistic expectations. Feldman and Newcomb (1973), after reviewing several studies on college choice, conclude that students base their college enrollment decision on nearness, cost, and some vague notion of academic excellence.

All of this suggests that the general expectations of students regarding college are ill-defined and often inaccurate. Yet these misconceptions and unrealistic expectations help to shape the college enrollment decision.

# INSTITUTIONAL CHARACTERISTICS

The personal characteristics of students clearly influence their college enrollment decisions. They are the most important variables in the determination to attend college or not. In the college-choice process, the institutional characteristics represent those variables that are more influential in determining what type of institution the student will attend and even the specific one (see Figure 7). Institutional characteristics include variables described as "fixed characteristics" by D. Chapman (1981). These encompass the location, the campus environment, the programs, the size, public versus private, and the relative price (high cost, moderate cost, or low cost) of the institution. Institutional factors also include fluid characteristics, which are the financial aid and pricing strategies, program alterations, and communication methods that individual colleges and universities practice.

## Fixed Characteristics

The fixed characteristics of an institution are usually central to the college's identity. Typically, there is little if anything the institution can do to alter them. The size and location of a university cannot normally be varied in any significant way, although some institutions have opened branch campuses as a means of changing their location(s). Many colleges would like to be able to increase their size, but with the declining numbers of high school graduates, most institutions are hoping simply to maintain enrollments.

Generally, the academic programs and the tuition levels of a college or university are inflexible. Private colleges may attempt to hold down costs, and community colleges are slowly raising their costs. Nevertheless, both groups will continue to be described as high- and low-cost institutions, respectively. In the same vein, some liberal arts colleges may develop more career-oriented programs such as computer science, and some polytechnical colleges may offer degrees in the humanities. Neither type of institution, however, is likely to successfully stray too far from its basic institutional strengths. Few religiously-affiliated colleges will shed their religious ties to become public or simply private institutions.

In an era of retrenchment, fixed characteristics can sound like a list of negative attributes that an institution is "stuck" with. This is seldom the case. The fixed characteristics of a college or university usually represent its uniqueness and are those qualities that differentiate one campus from another. Although many institutions might wish for larger endowments, more students, or a more generous taxing district, few would really choose to alter many of these fixed characteristics even if they could.

## Fluid Characteristics

Not all institutional characteristics are fixed. Colleges and universities can alter their financial aid and pricing policies. Alterations can be made in academic and student life programs, and strategies for institutional communication with students, parents, and other constituencies can be varied. These represent the institution's fluid characteristics. Chapter 4 is devoted to financial aid and pricing strategies, so these concerns will not be discussed at this time. Changes in academic programs and in student life can result in program reorganization or the development of new programs. The methods colleges use to communicate with students and other constituencies can take a number of forms; communication is probably the area in which the greatest amount of creativity and experimentation is taking place.

## INFLUENCING COLLEGE CHOICE

### Program Alteration

The academic programs of a university, and to a lesser extent the student life programs, are important when students reach the point of selecting which college to attend. Academic programs, in addition to cost and location, are probably the most influential institutional factors in the decision to attend a specific college or university. Few institutions can change their entire academic offerings, but program alterations are possible.

One form of program alteration most often attempted is the enhancement of academic program quality. A classic example is the honors program implemented at Swarthmore at the turn of the century. The honors program proved very successful and helped elevate Swarthmore's academic image substantially. Honors programs have since been created at colleges and universities around the country. National Merit Scholarship programs, special independent study programs, and undergraduate research opportunities are just a few examples of methods institutions have used to enhance the perceived quality of their academic offerings.

Often departments can be reorganized so that they are more relevant and marketable. For instance, history and political science might become a program in public policy analysis. English, theater arts, and speech could become a program in communication arts. Liberal arts colleges can make a strong case that no one can any longer be considered truly "educated" without courses in computer science. A strong polytechnical institution might consider integrating technical programs with a business degree or with an emphasis on technical writing. Such forms of program alteration can be accomplished without changing the basic mission of an institution and sometimes with little or no additional costs.

In addition to innovations in academic progams, some organizational changes in the student life area can be initiated to improve a college's drawing power. The University of California at San Diego decided to de-emphasize intercollegiate athletics and put more funds into its intramural programs. This was done to sharpen its image as a strong academic institution. The College of St. Francis in Joliet, Illinois, developed a stronger student life program at a time when many institutions were making cuts in this area. This was done to strengthen its ability to attract students who were looking for a small college with a good residential and student life program. Some universities have chosen to expand and strengthen their intercollegiate athletic programs as a means of attracting students who wish to participate in athletics, thus increasing their institutional visibility in the hope of attracting more students. Program alterations in either academics or student life can be viable methods for influencing student choice.

## Assessing the Competition

Those charged with the responsibility of managing enrollments will need to thoroughly understand which institutions are their chief competitors. They will have to discover what attracts some of their potential matriculants to other colleges and universities. Kotler, in his book *Marketing for Non-Profit Organizations* (1975), points out the need for a college to examine the kinds of programs and marketing activities that are being developed by competing colleges and universities on an ongoing basis. How do these institutions treat potential applicants? How much personal attention do the applicants receive? What are the institutions' pricing and financial aid policies? In addition, Kotler recommends that organizations regularly look at their own systems and procedures—even have someone go through the process as a potential matriculant—so that enrollment managers can see if their own rhetoric matches reality. At most institutions this is one area where much work remains to be done.

Many admissions personnel have never carefully collected information on students who applied, but did not attend, to determine whether they eventually went to college. In addition, those managers who have collected such data may not have analyzed it in sufficient detail. Simply looking at the ranking of those institutions that are most often listed on a cross-application list may not reveal the major competitors of a college or university. A given student may apply to one college, "just to see if I can get in," and another, "just in case I can't afford to go anyplace else."

The degree to which students consider public and private colleges in the same choice set is difficult to determine. Results from the work of Ghali, Miklius, and Wada (1977) and Maguire and Lay (1981) indicate that students seldom substitute public four-year higher education for private four-year higher education. Litten, Sullivan, and Brodigan (1983) and Zemsky and Oedel (1983), however, do describe some competition between the public and private sectors. Litten, Sullivan, and Brodigan write that almost 50 percent of the students in their research who listed a private college or university as the best institution also included public schools on their lists of institutions being considered. Nevertheless, 51 percent of all the students listed private colleges as their first and second choices (p. 63). In their research Zemsky and Oedel focus on a limited geographical area in New England. They find that (1) at the local level there is competition between public and private institutions; (2) at the regional level publics tend to compete with other publics and privates with other privates; (3) for students considering a national choice set of institutions, there is some competition between highly selective private and public flagship universities, but that the private institutions are more numerous.

At the two-year college level, Ghali, Miklius, and Wada also indicate that students usually do not substitute public community colleges for public four-year colleges. Similarly, Peters (1977) notes that over 80 percent of those planning to enter four-year colleges do so, and that over 60 percent of those planning to enroll in community colleges follow through on those plans (p. 11). Zemsky and Oedel point out, however, that one of the difficulties they encountered in studying college choice at community colleges is that students often do not have their test scores sent to two-year institutions because the scores are not required. This makes assessing the level of competition among the two-year and four-year sectors more difficult.

The mixed and contradictory results on substitutions among two- and four-year as well as public and private institutions illustrate some of the difficulties in understanding the college-choice process at the individual campus level. Such results make the case for the kind of institutional research programs conducted by Carleton College (Litten, Sullivan, and Brodigan 1983). These programs are essential if colleges and universities are to understand their market segments accurately and serve those populations effectively. These are examples of the type of research in which effective enrollment managers should be engaged. Enrollment managers will need to carefully analyze their marketing and recruitment activities and those of their competition. They will need to evaluate their activities on a regular and systematic basis to influence future enrollments.

# COLLEGE CHOICE: MAKING A DIFFERENCE

## Applying Choice Research

Although a number of factors influence college choice, most of them cannot be influenced readily by enrollment managers. A comprehensive understanding of college choice, however, does identify those areas upon which there is the greatest potential for enrollment managers to have an effect. Jackson (1982), after examining the variables that influence college choice, developed a chart he uses to evaluate the efficacy of various recruitment strategies. Table 1 depicts Jackson's work.

Of particular note in Table 1 is Jackson's emphasis on focus and latitude. Both concepts evaluate the efficacy of recruitment strategies in reaching students who could be the most greatly influenced by the appropriate tactic. In an earlier publication Jackson describes three types of high school graduates (1978, p. 571): The "whiches" are those students who will defi-

Table 1.  Evaluating the Efficiency of Recruitment Tactics

| Tactic | Target Factor | Intermediary | Effect | Cost | Focus* | Latitude† | Efficiency | Potential |
|---|---|---|---|---|---|---|---|---|
| School quality | academic experience | school | strong | high | low | moderate | low | low |
| College offerings | college characteristics | college | moderate | high | low | moderate | low | low |
| College location | location | college | strong | high | low | low | low | low |
| Academic help | academic experience | none | strong | moderate | high | high | high | high |
| Public subsidy | college costs | college | strong | moderate | low | moderate | moderate | low |
| General aid | college costs | none | strong | moderate | low | moderate | moderate | low |
| Targeted aid | college costs | none | strong | moderate | moderate | high | moderate | moderate |
| General information | information | none | moderate | low | low | low | moderate | low |
| Specific information | information | none | moderate | low | high | moderate | high | moderate |

* Focus is the ability of the tactic to concentrate efforts on students whose decisions are likely to be unsatisfactory without intervention.
† Latitude refers to the number of students whose decisions might be changed because of the intervention.
Source: Gregory Jackson 1982. *Educational Evaluation and Policy Analysis* 4(2): 239.

nitely attend a college or university; the only question is where they will attend. The "whethers" are those who are considering pursuing higher education but are also considering noneducational options. Typically, this group would be considering only one college or university. Third, the "nots" are those high school graduates who are not planning to continue their formal education. This group is not likely to be induced to attend an institution of higher learning. Jackson's evaluation of recruitment strategies, although general in nature, is especially sensitive to the "whethers" and the "nots."

Table 1 illustrates the difficulty for enrollment managers at individual institutions. Most of the tactics are either too inefficient or too expensive for an individual institution to undertake. Certain tactics do stand out, however, as holding some promise for individual institutions. Academic help, targeted aid, and general and specific information appear to have a moderate to high potential for influencing enrollments, as well as being at least moderately efficient in terms of latitude and focus. In addition, the cost of these activities is moderate to low.

For enrollment managers the ability to identify the appropriate market segments and then to inform and motivate them to matriculate relies on their ability to link marketing and recruitment practices to key variables in the college-choice process. For instance, if parents play an important role in the college choice, their influence is likely to be a cumulative one, not a onetime event that occurs during the senior year. In applying this research, consortiums of private church-related colleges may discover that developing a quarterly publication that reaches the parents of potential matriculants at an early age is an effective way to stimulate the primary demand for religiously-affiliated higher education. These institutions may discover that they would all benefit in the long run from the increased interest in religiously-affiliated colleges and universities, each member of the consortium gaining prospective matriculants over time. The capability of identifying different market segments and then field-testing written materials with samples of these segments, before actually sending them out en masse, may enhance the effectiveness of these materials. A strong institutional commitment to academic assistance programs, in conjunction with the recruitment of students who need and can benefit from such programs, offers yet another approach to communicating institutional strengths to students in order to influence their choice. Obviously, tuition levels and financial aid can influence the enrollment decision. Discussion of these factors will follow in Chapter 4.

In the future, enrollment managers will need to be able to draw pragmatic links between research on college choice and recruitment and marketing activities. Table 2 offers a systematic approach for making such linkages.

In Table 2 one dimension of the college choice—the role of significant others—has been paired with enrollment strategies and then evaluated. Some strategies hold more promise than do others. The effort to communicate with parents has already been discussed. Another strategy that holds some promise is that of linking the role of friends with targeted peer recruitment. Almost any admissions office can point to certain areas from which they consistently draw students with very little effort. One of the variables that is probably in operation in these settings is that of peers influencing each other. A good market survey should be able to identify other communities or regions where high school students have the kinds of characteristics that suggest they might find attending a particular institution attractive, but for some reason have not considered it. By targeting these areas in recruitment efforts and financial aid awards, an institution could develop the kind of peer reputation, over time, that would eventually produce a consistent flow of matriculants from those areas.

Focusing on the roles of parents and friends is just one example of using research on college choice to develop more effective approaches to recruitment. For at least the next 10 to 15 years, efforts to integrate research, planning, and effective marketing will be crucial for many institutions of higher learning.

Enrollment managers need to be engaged in a continuing cycle that links

1. personal and institutional variables
2. with campus-based research
3. to develop strategies for recruitment that
4. should then be continually evaluated.

Table 2. Evaluating the Linkages between Choice Variables and Enrollment Strategies

| Linkages | | Evaluation | | |
|---|---|---|---|---|
| *Choice Variables* | *Enrollment Strategies* | *Cost* | *Potential* | *Efficiency** |
| Significant Others | | | | |
| 1. Parents | 1a. Written materials | low | moderate (long-range) | moderate |
| | 1b. Parent campus visit | low | low | low |
| 2. Friends | 2a. Peer recruitment | low | moderate | low |
| | 2b. Targeted peer recruitment | moderate | moderate/high | moderate |
| 3. High school conselors | 3a. Counselor newsletter | low | low | low |
| | 3b. High school visit | moderate | low | low |
| | 3c. Campus visits for counselors | low/moderate | low | low |

* Efficieny: cost/potential ratio.

The linking of strategies with research and the evaluation of the potential of these strategies are essential for effective enrollment management.

## Tools for Investigating College Choice

An increasing number of resources are available for enrollment managers who wish to understand more clearly the factors that influence college choice as the process relates to a specific institution. Perhaps the most exciting resource to emerge recently is the Enrollment Planning Service developed by the College Board. The Enrollment Planning Service (the product of the project that led to Zemsky and Oedel's work *The Structure of College Choice,* 1983), gives individual colleges and universities access to information regarding cross-applications by institutional type. Not only can institutions receive aggregate information about the characteristics of their market, but the service includes software that enables campuses to analyze the data in ways most useful for their individual needs. This can assist enrollment managers in developing a more accurate picture of cross-application trends and in analyzing market conditions.

In addition to this newest resource, there are others. The College Board, in conjunction with the National Center for Higher Education Management Systems (NCHEMS), makes available an Entering Student Questionnaire as part of their Student Outcomes Information Service. The American College Testing Program (ACT) markets two surveys, the Survey of Postsecondary Plans and the Entering Student Survey. The first is for high school seniors, the second for college matriculants. The two ACT instruments and the College Board/NCHEMS questionnaire can provide enrollment managers with useful information about the characteristics and expectations of traditional-age college students. The ACE/UCLA Freshman Survey, conducted by the Cooperative Institutional Research Program at the Institute of Higher Education at the University of California at Los Angeles, can provide important information about entering students and how they compare with fellow students at a wide variety of campuses. The College Board also offers the Student Descriptive Questionnaire, which provides information on the characteristics of new students. The Board also publishes a *Summary Report* of the results of these questionnaires, as well as an annual *Profile,* which describes all students who take the SAT. Finally, the ACT Student Report includes useful data on student plans, expectations, and career orientations. This report provides a comprehensive view of entering students. In some sense these resources help enrollment managers to see their institutions through the eyes of prospective matriculants. Each tool can provide information that will enable enrollment managers to develop a better understanding of the factors that influence the student's choice.

## The Research Agenda

The research agenda for enrollment managers is exciting. Although a great deal of work has already been done on college choice, very little attention has been paid to how a potential matriculant finally chooses a specific institution. On a more applied level, enrollment planners must have a complete profile of both their applicants and their matriculants. They must be able to:

1. Describe the socioeconomic characteristics of their students and their applicants.
2. Describe the communities and types of high schools that their applicants and matriculants come from.
3. Provide a profile of the academic skills and abilities of their applicants and matriculants.
4. Understand the goals and aspirations of those students who matriculate and those who do not.
5. Characterize the expectations of college that matriculants bring with them.

Integrating this kind of institutional data with college-choice research and appropriate recruitment strategies can enhance the efforts of enrollment managers.

## SUGGESTIONS FOR FURTHER READING

"A Model of Student College Choice," by David Chapman.
*Toward a Theory of College Choice: A Model of College Search and Choice Behavior,* by R. G. Chapman.
"Public Efficiency and Private Choice in Higher Education," by Gregory Jackson.
"Different Strokes in the Applicant Pool: Some Refinements in a Model of Student Choice," by Larry Litten.
*Applying Market Research in College Admissions,* by Larry Litten, Daniel Sullivan, and David Brodigan.
*College Choice in America,* by Charles Manski and David Wise.
*The Structure of College Choice,* by Robert Zemsky and Penney Oedel.

# Chapter 4

# Pricing and Financial Aid

## DOLLARS AND STUDENTS

A discussion of pricing and financial aid brings Part One, a review of student demand for higher education and research on college choice, to a natural conclusion. As described in Chapter 2, the net price of higher education does have some effect on the demand. In general, however, the aggregate demand for college places appears to be relatively unresponsive to price. Nevertheless, the net cost of attending a college does influence the choice process. Perhaps nothing has done more to highlight the importance of tuition and financial aid than recent public policy shifts. At the national level, reductions in the funding levels of student aid programs and an uncertain future have created anxieties for students and institutions alike. At the state level, allocations for student aid programs have generally leveled off, and in some cases there have been actual reductions in student assistance programs.

Until recently, financial aid programs have steadily grown in terms of their total monetary value as well as in their importance to students and institutions of higher learning. The National Task Force on Student Aid has noted that the amount of assistance to students has increased sixty-sixfold between 1960 and 1980 (Jensen 1981, p. 280). From 1970 to 1980 the federal investment in financial aid grew from 1 billion dollars to 5 billion dollars (St. John and Byce 1982, p. 24).

Despite this large increase in student assistance, the purposes and goals of student aid programs remain muddled and ambiguous. The aims of financial aid programs, including federal, state, and institutional assistance, are not clearly articulated. Herndon (1982) concludes:

> Over the years student aid has been used to assist needy students, expand student choice, to reward past assistance to society (veterans), to ensure the survival of educational institutions, to meet demand for skilled laborers, to remedy past racial injustice, and most recently to address broader political objectives such as financial relief for middle income students (p. 38).

In addition, this list should include student achievement, student retention, and the discouragement of out-of-state migration of students. Depending on one's loyalties and perspective, student assistance programs have been seen as an absolute necessity or an overly generous subsidy.

Initially, the purpose of campus-based financial aid programs was to assist needy students and to permit colleges and universities to attract students with desirable characteristics and abilities. State and federal programs began to help assure access for all qualified students. Gradually, the concerns for access shifted to an interest in choice. Not only should students be assured of access to a college or university, but they should be assured of being able to attend the institution of their choice regardless of cost. More recently, with the enactment of the Middle Income Assistance Act, the focus of federal programs shifted from choice to "comfort," which is the notion that students and parents should be able to pursue the college education of their choice without too much sacrifice. The policies of the Reagan administration, however, have clearly marked a shift back toward choice and perhaps even access.

Throughout all the shifts in public policy and campus-based aid programs, many institutions have demonstrated they lack a consistent philosophical or theoretical base for financial aid programs. At the federal and state levels, competing political forces have created a system that purports to meet student need, but in actuality appears to simply ration scarce financial aid resources. At the institutional level, very little data-based research has been conducted, and many financial aid directors make awards mechanically on a first-come, first-served basis rather than on the basis of well-defined goals and objectives.

In the following pages the role of pricing and financial aid in the enrollment decision is examined. The impact of increases and decreases in net price are reviewed, as well as questions of whether tuition decreases or financial aid increases have a stronger effect on attendance. In addition, different kinds of financial aid and their effectiveness in different sectors of the higher education system are analyzed.

These issues are reviewed in conjunction with trends in financing a college education. Awarding patterns and the criteria for making financial aid awards are examined along with some current strategies being developed to make maximum use of tuition policies and financial aid awards. Finally, ethical issues in financial aid and pricing are discussed.

## PRICING AND CHOICE

The notion that students carefully weigh the net price of several institutions before determining which college they will attend is a myth. Fewer than one-third of all college applicants have more than one option in terms of college choice (Corwin and Kent 1978, p. 3). Since most students apply to only one college, they are not in a position to weigh the net price of two or more colleges or universities. As a result, many students eliminate some colleges and apply to one or more on the basis of what they perceive to be the cost, usually the "list price."

Even in terms of the one institution that most students apply to, few applicants have a good idea of what the actual cost of attendance will be. In most cases students do not discover what the actual net cost of attending will be until after they apply, are accepted, and then are awarded financial aid. Thus, most students make their application decision on the basis of the list price of one college or university (Elliott 1980; Corwin and Kent 1978; The College Board 1976).

This is not to imply that financial aid plays no role in the enrollment decision. Students are sensitive to net price when they are choosing between two or more colleges (Hearn 1980; Jackson 1978). According to Jackson, receiving aid is actually more important than the amount received. Similarly, Manski and Wise (1983) discovered a .86 correlation between receiving aid and attendance (p. 101). The evidence points to the importance of financial aid in influencing college choice.

Although both tuition and financial aid play a role in the college choice, as a result of student application patterns, tuition is more influential than financial aid, or net price, in terms of its impact on the application decision (Elliott 1980; Hearn 1980; Hyde 1977; Jackson and Weathersby 1975). These facts, which are often overlooked, have implications for financial aid and pricing policies that will be returned to later in this chapter.


## TUITION VERSUS AID

Another method of weighing the relationship between college attendance and price is to examine the effect of raising or lowering tuition against the impact of increasing financial aid. Several studies have tried to measure carefully the effects of tuition increases. Depending on the income level of the family (lower income families are more responsive to price changes), research suggests decreases in enrollment ranging from 0.7 to 3.26 percent will follow a $100 increase in tuition (Campbell and Siegel 1967; Hoenack 1971; National Commission on Financing Postsecondary Education 1973; Radner and Miller 1970). Corrazzini, Dugan, and Grabowski (1972) note that a $100 decrease in tuition results in a 2.65 percent increase in enrollments (p. 47). Stampen (1980) monitored an experiment in the University of Wisconsin system in which tuitions at selected institutions within the system were lowered by 50 percent (over $300). He found that the decrease resulted in increases in enrollments ranging from 16.1 to 32 percent (p. 95).

In the only other actual case of substantial increases or decreases in tuition, Stampen describes a 15 percent drop in enrollments at the City University of New York (p. 41). This occurred in 1976 when a fiscal crisis forced the CUNY system to charge tuitions of $700 or more. Before this time there had been no tuition at the CUNY colleges. Not surprisingly, most of the decline was seen in the lowest income groups. In actual situations, however, it is difficult to measure the true impact of tuition changes because many of these CUNY students were now eligible for increased financial aid, which reduced the impact of the tuition increases.

Jackson and Weathersby (1975) re-analyzed the data from most of these studies and others, using a consistent methodological approach. The authors demonstrate that a $100 increase in tuition results in a decrease in enrollments ranging from 0.06 to 1.9 percent (p. 647). Dickmeyer, Wessels, and Goldren (1981) state that a $100 cut in tuition would result in a 1 percent increase in enrollment (p. 48). Manski and Wise (1983) after a thorough study of the National Longitudinal Study of the Class of 1972, conclude that the negative value of an increase in tuition and the positive value of a similar increase in scholarship aid (grants, not loans or work-study) are approximately equal in terms of their impact on enrollments (p. 9). They also state that the negative value of an increase in room and board costs is about the same as the negative value of an increase in tuition costs (p. 9). Manski and Wise are careful to point out, however, that these results do not hold true for community colleges. For community colleges, their results and those of Zucker and Nazari-Robati (1982) suggest that the positive value of financial aid is worth considerably more that the negative value of increased tuition.

Research concerning the impact of tuition and financial aid on enrollments reveals that the relative value placed on tuition decreases as opposed to financial aid increases is about equal. These findings do not, however, resolve the problem of making students aware of their net cost before the application decision. Nevertheless, the results may have some utility for residential colleges and community colleges. Some residential colleges and universities attempt each year to alternate large increases in tuition with those in room and board. They do this in the belief that students will not respond as negatively as they would to increases in both. The preceding discussion implies that this may be a fruitless tactic because students react similarly to either increase. The findings also point out that community colleges need to give financial aid policies and the administration of financial aid offices careful attention; financial aid is important to community college students.

## STUDENTS, INSTITUTIONS, AND PRICE

Thus far, most of our discussion has examined the role of pricing in aggregate terms. Tuition and financial aid policies, however, do not affect students or institutions equally. To manage enrollments, decision makers must be able to anticipate how changes in net pricing will affect student enrollment. The impact of tuition increases and decreases, as well as changes in financial aid policies across various sectors of the United States higher education system, will now be analyzed.

### Pricing and Students

Although public community colleges are the lowest cost institutions of higher learning in this country, they are, paradoxically, the most vulnerable to enrollment shifts based on pricing policies. For many students community colleges are "borderline" institutions where significant numbers of potential students are considering noneducational alternatives such as employment, the military, or working in the home. In Jackson's words (see Applying Choice Research above), community colleges attract the "whethers" and some of the "nots." Increases or decreases in net cost affect these groups much more than they do those considering options from among several educational opportunities—the "whiches." Berne (1980) states that a $100 increase in financial aid for potential matriculants considering a noneducational alternative will increase their chances of attending by 3.5 percent (p. 407). Hyde (1977) describes many of those considering community colleges as a "captive market" that is very cost-sensitive (p. 10). Berne (1980), after looking at a number of factors that influence enrollments at two-year colleges, concludes that net price is the single variable that is robust across all estimates of attendance (p. 407).

The effects of changes in the net cost at four-year colleges, both public and private, are more subtle. As ability and family income rise, the likelihood of a student's attending a four-year institution increases. As ability and family income continue to increase, the chances that a student will select a private college or university rises. In addition, as the socioeconomic status of the student increases, the importance of student aid decreases. Hyde notes that as tuition increases in the public sector, more students of high socioeconomic status will switch to the private sector. Conversely, among private institutions, tuition increases do not affect the enrollment rates of high-income students as negatively as they do middle-income students.

Women are generally more price-responsive than men are, but women of low socioeconomic background at private colleges and universities are less price-responsive than are their male counterparts (Feldman and Hoenack 1969). Feldman and Hoenack also conclude that high-ability males are less sensitive to price increases at all socioeconomic levels. Hyde looks at the price responsiveness of potential attenders who are high-income, middle-income, low-income, or below the poverty level. He asserts that high-income and low-income students are the least sensitive to changes in price, and that middle-income and below-poverty-level students are the most sensitive to increases or decreases in cost. This phenomenon may be the result of the apparent middle-income squeeze (which will be discussed later in this chapter) and the fact that the very poor are extremely sensitive to the opportunity costs of higher education. The very poor may also believe they cannot afford postsecondary education at any cost.

## Financial Aid and Institutions

In the United States a complex and varied system of scholarships, grants, loans, and work-study programs has evolved, which is superimposed on a system of federal, state, and campus-based financial aid programs. It is not surprising to discover that these various forms of financial aid appear to be more heavily used within different sectors of the higher education system.

Once again, beginning with the community college system, it appears that Pell Grants have had the greatest impact on enrollments at the two-year college level (The Carnegie Council on Policy Studies on Higher Education 1979; Manski and Wise 1983). Manski and Wise document a 59 percent increase in the enrollment rates of low-income students and a 12 percent increase in the college-going rates of middle-income students. The authors note that these enrollment gains are "totally concentrated at two-year and vocational schools" (p. 125). Manski and Wise further speculate that many of those who do not pursue postsecondary schooling would have to be paid to be induced to enroll. For some students this may be perceived to be precisely the case when a community college matriculant receives a Pell Grant that covers tuition and some living expenses as well. Community college students generally do not need to take loans, nor would many be inclined to do so. Low-income students and those of less ability are usually hesitant to take student loans and will often not pursue a higher education alternative that would necessitate using loan funds.

College matriculants attending public and private four-year colleges and universities typically rely on a broader mix of financial aid. Students in both the public and private sectors make use of federal, state, and institutional grants and scholarships. Although students in private colleges and universities are somewhat more likely to receive gift money, large numbers in both sectors are awarded gift money (Boyd et al. 1978; The Carnegie Council on Policy Studies on Higher Education 1979; Hyde 1977). Differences in the mix of financial aid are more apparent when loans and college work-study awards are examined. Students entering private institutions are much more likely to use loans to finance their educations (Boyd et al. 1978; The Carnegie Council on Policy Studies on Higher Education 1979; Hyde 1977). In fact, between 1967 and 1977, Boyd et al. document a decline of more than 50 percent in the willingness of matriculants at state colleges in Illinois to accept loans. The authors note a decline of approximately 19 percent in the number of students at private colleges and universities who accepted loans during the same 10-year period (p. 6). Between 1978 and 1980 the percentage of low-income students utilizing the Guaranteed Student Loan Program also fell from 25 to 20.5 percent (U.S. Department of Education 1981, p. 387). Most of this decrease was made up with an increase in Pell Grants to these low-income groups. Students in the private sector are also more likely to use work-study dollars or money earned in part-time jobs while in school to help pay for the costs of their education (Boyd et al. 1978; Hyde 1977). The differences in work-study participation between students in the public and private institutions, however, are not nearly so pronounced (Boyd et al. 1978; Hyde 1977).

The results of this discussion suggest that student access to loans is of great importance to the private sector. High interest rates, stiffer income eligibility requirements, or reductions in the amount of money available for loans could have a negative impact on enrollments in private colleges and universities.

## FINANCING A COLLEGE EDUCATION

As the price of attending an institution of higher education rose during the last decade, concerns over the availability of the consumers of higher education—parents and matriculants—to pay for the increasing costs mounted. The plight of the middle-income student, in particular, became a major political issue. With the emphasis on access and choice for low-income students and the ability of high-income students to pursue higher education regardless of financial aid policies, growing attention was focused on the middle-income family. Many public policy analysts, politicians, educators, and middle-income families themselves began to fear that they were becoming priced out of private higher education, and perhaps even out of some state-supported institutions.

On one side of this debate economists argued that there was no "middle-income squeeze" (Corwin and Kent 1978). Those who insisted that there was no middle-income squeeze asserted that family disposable income after taxes had kept pace with, or exceeded, increases in tuition. It was also believed that financial aid forms had allowed parents to underestimate the value of their houses and other possessions so that they appeared less affluent. Research conducted by Augenblick and Hyde (1979) found that middle-income students at state-supported colleges had their needs over-met, while those at private institutions were receiving enough aid to meet their needs. Conversely, they found that the parents of low-income students were contributing $200 to $300 more than they were expected to (pp. 81–82).

Presenting a contrasting view were those who asserted that middle-income families were indeed being priced out of some options in the United States system of higher education (Glover 1978; Van Alstyne 1979). Glover noted that middle-income parents had to take greater pro-portional cuts in their standard of living than did low-income parents. Van Alstyne argued that most studies of the middle-income family underesti-mated their plight because they used aggregate data. Her data suggested that between 1969 and 1971, when inflation and taxes were taken into consideration, tuition had risen faster at all types of institutions than the family median income had increased (p. 3). Van Alstyne found that dual career families were paying more payroll taxes and that the typical Amer-ican family now had children only three years apart (rather than four years, which had been used in calculations), which meant that many families had two children in a college or university at the same time (p. 2). In a more recent work, Frances (1983) writes: "Since 1980, college tuitions have gone up close to 40 percent, twice as fast as the median family income. . . ." (p. 4).[1]

Although the findings of Glover and Van Alstyne (later Frances) suggest that there is indeed a middle-income squeeze, a 1983 College Board Report shows that this is not the case. Gillespie and Carlson (1983) analyze trends in college costs, family income, and aid per full-time student and find that families have more resources from income and student aid relative to costs than they did in 1963–64. Most of this growth, however, took place before 1973–74 (p. vi). In constant 1982 dollars, the median level of aid per FTE student was $462 in 1963–64 compared with $1,693 in 1983–84 (p. 20).

[1] Van Alstyne and Frances are the same individual.

Perceptions, nevertheless, play an important role in this discussion. Since 1980, costs have increased in relation to aid and income (p. vi).

In any case, there can be little doubt that the Middle Income Student Assistance Act of 1980 (MISAA) was a response to the perceived problems of the middle-income family. Whether or not this ultimately proved to be a boon for higher education, and the private sector in particular, remains to be seen. Private colleges may be discovering that those middle-income families who had the opportunity to use subsidized interest terms of the Guaranteed Student Loan Program will not be willing to once again make the sacrifices necessary for them to send their sons and daughters to private institutions.

## STRATEGIES FOR FINANCIAL AID AND PRICING

Before the enabling legislation for the Pell Grants (formerly the Basic Educational Opportunity Grants) in 1972, discretionary campus-based financial aid was an important part of any student assistance program. With the passage of MISAA in 1980, it appeared as though access, choice, and perhaps even "comfort" were assured for all potential college attenders. This illusion was short-lived. Current federal policies and shortfalls in state revenues have once again made student assistance and pricing policies at the campus level a critical concern for many institutions. Colleges and universities must assess their policies and procedures for awarding federal, state, and campus-based financial aid. This section explores the research agenda essential for enrollment managers if they are to make the maximum use of their student assistance programs, and also discusses some current strategies for effectively using financial aid and tuition policies to enhance the net revenue per enrolled student.

### The Research Agenda

Many financial aid officers resist using student assistance as a recruiting device; yet this is probably a key element of any enrollment management strategy. To use student assistance effectively, however, the institution must develop a set of goals and objectives, a philosophy of financial assistance for students. Enrollment managers must lead the institution in the development of goals that address the characteristics of the student body along the following dimensions: student quality, kinds of students, numbers of students, and net tuition revenues.

Often enrollment managers will discover that there is no institutional data base for developing such priorities. Without such information it is difficult to determine if campus financial aid packages really make a difference. Without a careful evaluation of the impact of financial aid policies, a college or university may be overawarding some segments of its student market, thus not reaping the maximum benefit of the awards. On the other hand, some institutions may be underawarding and therefore not converting as many applicants into matriculants as they might.

Dickmeyer, Wessels, and Goldren (1981) propose a seven-step "iterative pricing model":

1. The institution must first project the potential student market-by-market.
2. The institution must estimate its segment-by-segment share of the market in relation to other educational institutions and commercial employers.
3. As part of an overall marketing plan, an institution must estimate the responsiveness of potential students from each market segment to changes in the institution's net tuition level for that segment.
4. The institution must project enrollment levels by segment under three or four possible net tuition strategies.
5. Federal, state, and campus-based aid must then be allocated in each of the proposed strategies based on the stated tuition for that strategy.
6. The strategies must be evaluated to determine whether the projected tuition revenue and aid expenditures result in a balanced budget.
7. The tuition and financial aid policy variations must be compared to determine which of the strategies, or combination thereof, will result in the best budgetary and enrollment assumptions for the institution (pp. 3–8).

Most admissions offices routinely collect data on each entering class. This information is usually transformed into an admissions profile of each class. Enrollment managers, however, also need to develop financial aid profiles of the student body. This profile should answer several questions: How much aid is distributed to which students? At what rate are the incomes of students' families changing each year and how is this related to the amount of aid they are receiving? How are the students' sources of support changing over time? How much are people authorized to borrow and how much do they borrow? Are any income groups underrepresented (this may indicate over- and underawarding)? Are awards made where they really make a difference? What is the relationship between academic success and financial aid? How does the financial aid profile compare with the admissions profile or the institutional retention profile? Clearly, there is a full agenda of research for enrollment managers in the area of tuition and financial aid.

## Pricing Strategies

The research agenda in pricing should enable enrollment managers to develop more sophisticated and effective strategies for setting tuition and awarding financial aid. Within the last few years a number of proposals and suggestions have emerged to enhance institutional pricing structures. Authors such as Ihlanfeldt (1980) and Weinberg (1978) have discussed targeted pricing strategies in which tuition costs are varied according to the student's grade level, by the department, on the basis of cost per unit, or on the basis of pricing by term. Depending on the college and the program, any one of these strategies may be viable. The guaranteed cost concept is also finding its way back into favor among some institutions. Administrators at Gustavus Adolphus College in St. Peter, Minnesota, believe that this plan not only attracts students to the college but, perhaps even more important, helps to keep the attrition rate extremely low.

Although few colleges and universities would opt for the guaranteed cost plan, it is possible that some institutions may find it effective actually to reduce the stated cost and campus-based aid. If most students make the decision to apply on the basis of the list price, some of the less prestigious private colleges and state colleges may discover that they can no longer continue to raise tuition levels in an era when inflation appears to be slowing and federal and state aid funds are no longer increasing. They may discover that increases in costs will actually result in lower net tuition revenues. Eureka College in Eureka, Illinois, has been taking this tactic—lowering the net price for those students who live in their primary market.

Along with innovative ideas for tuition policies, there are also many proposals for making more effective use of financial aid resources. Hodgkinson (1982) suggests a number of ways to stretch financial aid dollars. Among her more promising ideas are such concepts as increasing the parental contribution required or enlarging the amount of self-help asked of each matriculant; establishing a "rolling" financial aid schedule during which in the first 60 days 90 percent of need might be met, followed by 80 percent during the next 60 days, and so forth; creating a targeted aid grid that graphically charts award priorities and goals; establishing a quota of need-blind awards; and targeting institutional money for work-study and loans. Hodgkinson also describes the Beloit Plan—a tax deductible loan program (p. 47). Hauptman (1982) describes institutional strategies for working with loans. For example, colleges and universities may enter into agreements with lending institutions to create their own loan programs, pay Guaranteed Student Loan origination fees, pay part of the Parent's Loan for Undergraduate Students (PLUS) program costs, or even subsidize the interest rates of these federal loan programs (p. 75).

In addition to these various options, the importance of effective methods to communicate the net price of attending a given college or university should not be underestimated. Written materials, targeted to each market segment and giving a picture of the true cost of enrolling, would provide students with more accurate information as they narrow their choice set. Earlier notification of financial aid awards should also enhance the pricing policies of the institution. Packer (1980) notes that as recently as 1979, 49 percent of those students coming from families with incomes of less than $6,000 did not apply for financial aid because they did not believe they were eligible (p. 80). *Making It Count* (1976), published by the College Board, also verifies that perceived "list cost," rather than actual information, affects student choice. *Student Aid and the Urban Poor* (The College Board, 1981) documents the need for better counseling and more and better information about higher education for disadvantaged students. Although both of these last citations speak to the needs of low-income students, based on much of the research described in Chapters 3 and 4, these same statements could be extrapolated to a lesser degree for more affluent students as well. These efforts are part of the communication strategies discussed in Chapter 3 and are also an important part of an institutional marketing plan.

Pricing policies are significant in any enrollment management plan. As competition for students increases in the next 15 years, tuition levels and financial aid will become even more crucial to the health and vitality of many colleges and universities. Careful planning, research, and evaluation will be key elements in successful enrollment management efforts.

## ETHICAL CONSIDERATIONS

Enrollment management carries with it an implied emphasis on productivity, efficiency, and results. Indeed, with such an approach it might be possible to develop an enrollment plan that effectively allocates financial aid with no thought to issues of equity or access. Colleges and universities do need to be managed more effectively, but they do not exist only to sell a product. Enrollment managers must take into consideration the mission of the institution as well as concerns for a more equitable and democratic society. In the United States access to education at all levels is associated with equality.

### Access

Recently the efficacy of the billions of dollars spent by the federal government to assure access and choice has been questioned. In August 1982,

W. Lee Hansen, an economist at the University of Wisconsin, issued a research report that suggested these federal programs had failed. Hansen asserted there had been no change "in the ratio of college enrollment rates for youth from families with income below the median relative to youth from families with above median incomes" (p. I). Furthermore he cited data from 1972 and 1980 surveys that revealed there had been no real change in the matriculation plans of high school seniors during this time when socioeconomic status and ability were controlled.

At a time when the federal government appears to be pulling back from its commitment to choice, and perhaps access, the report seems to give support to trends at the federal level. Shortly after Hansen's results were made public, however, several critiques of his work appeared. Comments from two of these critiques (Breneman 1982; El-Khawas and Henderson 1982) make clear that Hansen's work will not be the final word on this subject. (Nor, in fairness to Hansen, did he intend it to be; he too raises several questions and concerns about his results at the end of his paper.) Briefly, some of the flaws in Hansen's paper are the following:

—The data include only the 18-to-24-age cohort of dependent students; 40 percent of all Pell Grant awards now go to independent students.

—The aggregate treatment of the two surveys masks the fact that there was a large increase between 1972 and 1980 in the numbers of lower income students who were interested in two-year programs and programs leading to professional degrees.

—The separation of income levels into two groups, those above and below the median income, do not accurately reflect the shifts among various subgroups of low-income students.

—The rates of comparison include years when draft laws may have kept enrollment rates artificially high; the fact that enrollment rates did not show large declines may be the result of increases in financial aid.

—In light of the large increases in tuition rates, federal aid may be responsible for the fact that enrollment rates did not decrease.

Hansen's paper and the subsequent responses raise a new set of questions for economists and public policymakers. For enrollment managers this debate is an important one they should observe carefully. They may find the need to speak articulately on these issues to various publics. In addition, issues of access should concern everyone associated with higher education, particularly enrollment managers.

## Equity

During the past two decades equality of opportunity has been one of the primary movers of public policy with regard to federal and state student assistance programs. The Three trends in this area need to be monitored closely by those concerned with collegiate enrollments: (1) the shift away from need-blind admissions policies, (2) the increasing importance of merit vis-à-vis need in financial aid awarding, and (3) the shift of larger amounts of Pell Grants and Supplemental Educational Opportunity Grant (SEOG) funds to middle- and high-income students.

Many institutions across the country had maintained financial aid policies that promised to meet the need of any student who was admitted. With the reductions in federal assistance programs in 1981, a number of these colleges and universities began to wonder if they would be able to continue to make such a promise (*Chronicle of Higher Education,* Nov. 3, 1982, p. 9). Although a recent College Board survey reveals that a shift away from need-blind admissions policies has not occurred yet, the results do show that many campuses have been reviewing these policies (Nelson 1984). Enrollment managers should monitor these trends closely.

Similarly, as the competition for students has intensified, more and more colleges and universities have had to use campus-based funds to make merit awards. Since institutional funds are finite, of necessity this practice reduces the amount of money available to meet the needs of other students who lack the special talents or characteristics the institution may desire. Manski and Wise (1983) conclude that merit is now weighted the same as need in most colleges. While it is unrealistic to expect many colleges and universities to unilaterally end merit awards and move to an entirely need-based policy, this does not mean that there is no alternative. Because there are not sufficient federal, state, and institutional funds to allocate money to all who need assistance, most colleges are forced to ration these scarce resources. Perhaps a workable compromise is a commitment on the part of each institution to a quota of need-blind awards to be made to high-need students each year. When these awards are made, the money is gone, but at least each institution will have made a conscious decision to aid some students who lack the kinds of skills that bring them merit awards yet have the desire to pursue higher learning at specific campuses.

Finally, there is a clear trend toward awarding more Pell Grants and SEOG funds to middle- and high-income students. Manski and Wise reveal that since the liberalization of the Pell Grant standards in 1979–80, the portion of these grants going to middle- and upper-income students reached 40 percent in 1980 (p. 119). In addition SEOG funds (which were originally provided to help meet the unmet need of those students requiring the greatest assistance) show an almost fivefold increase between 1974–75 and 1978–79 in the percentage of funds going to students with family incomes over $12,000 (St. John and Byce 1982, p. 27). It must be noted, however, that the liberalization in the standards was part of the Middle

Income Student Assistance Act, which was a response to the perceived middle-income squeeze. Dickmeyer, Wessels, and Goldren (1981) discuss this trend in Pell Grants and conclude that it is the result of a more equitable formula for middle-income students and a recognition of the increased numbers of multiple children in college at the same time.

Nevertheless, this shift should be monitored. Since colleges are rationing rather than allocating financial aid funds, dollars shifted away from low-income students are not likely to be replaced by other sources of assistance. The College Scholarship Service of the College Board, the National Association of College Admissions Counselors, and the Statement of Principals and Practice of Student Financial Aid Administrators call for financial aid to be need-based; yet there is strong evidence that this is increasingly less the case. This is an ethical dilemma that will not be resolved in the near future by more funds, by a failure to deal with the issue, or, with the exception of a few well-endowed schools with strong drawing power, by a belief that an individual institution, that awards all funds on the basis of need can afford to shift to a need-blind aid system. Each institution will have to grapple with this dilemma and find its own answer.

## THE NEED FOR APPLIED RESEARCH

Implementing a targeted financial aid system that is ethical and also attracts the kinds of students an institution seeks in sufficient numbers is not an easy task. Unlike some applied research conducted in the areas of college choice and student retention, research in pricing and financial aid has not attracted as much interest until recently. A College Board 1976 publication, *Making It Count: A Report on a Project to Provide Better Financial Aid Information to Students,* discusses the common flaws in the communication process regarding financial aid and the kinds of information students and parents report they need. The College Board makes available the Student Expense and Resource Survey (SEARS), which enables colleges and universities to collect and analyze information about how students pay for college. In addition student profiles available from the ACE/UCLA Freshman Survey, the American College Testing Program, and the College Board can at least provide some background information on applicants and matriculants.

Several colleges and universities have been recognized for their efforts in pricing and financial aid. Beloit College, Boston College, Carleton College, Northwestern University (under the leadership of William Ihlandfeldt), and St. Louis University have been acknowledged leaders in the private sector. Iowa State University has developed an effective data-based financial aid system in the large public sector. Will Chatam, at Johnson County Community College in Overland Park, Kansas, is highly regarded for his work in financial aid in community colleges.

The current problem in this area remains the lack of systematic research. For enrollment managers this is an issue of critical importance that will require increased inquiry.

## SUGGESTIONS FOR FURTHER READING

*Guide to the Literature of Student Financial Aid,* by Jerry S. Davis and William D. Van Dusen.

*Institutionally Funded Student Financial Aid,* by Nathan Dickmeyer, J. Wessels, and S. L. Goldren.

*Trends in Student Financial Aid: 1963 to 1983,* by Donald A. Gillespie and Nancy Carlson.

*New Directions for Institutional Research: The Impact of Student Financial Aid on Institutions,* by Joe B. Henry (ed.).

"Financial Aid and Educational Outcomes: A Review," by Eric Jensen.

*New Directions for Higher Education: Institutionally Funded Financial Aid in a Period of Retrenchment,* by Martin Kramer (ed.).

*College Choice in America,* by Charles Manski and David Wise.

# PART TWO

Part Two examines student-institution fit and student attrition. The two topics are inseparable. As will be seen, the literature on student-institution fit provides enrollment managers with an understanding of how the characteristics of a given campus and the qualities of the students create an environment. This environment in turn has an impact on both the students and the institution. Attracting students who are congruent with the college or university is a proactive approach to reducing the dropout rate.

Retention studies focus on factors related to student persistence. There is also a growing body of knowledge on retention programs. Since retaining currently enrolled students is much more cost-effective than recruiting students to replace dropouts, student attrition programs are a vital element of an enrollment management plan.

*Chapter 5*

---

# Recruiting Graduates: Understanding Student-Institution Fit

*Terry E. Williams*

## CONCEPTUALIZING STUDENT-INSTITUTION FIT

Enrollment management in higher education requires the effective managing of college enrollments from the point of initial student contact to the point of graduation and even beyond in facilitating alumni support for the enrollment management effort. Today most institutional leaders would agree that campus efforts to retain those students who enroll are just as vital to enrollment stability as efforts expended in attracting the students to the institution in the first place. This chapter is the first of two chapters focusing on the important issue of student retention. As Chapter 1 suggests, today the emerging profession of enrollment management must have a comprehensive understanding of many different enrollment-related concepts. Several of these concepts specifically relate to the vast amount of research and theory pertaining to the retention of students.

This chapter focuses on one of several important concepts related to retention: *student-institution fit.* A growing body of knowledge that is both research- and theory-based strongly suggests that the degree of congruency, or fit, between student needs, abilities, interests, and goals and the ability of the institution to adequately respond to those needs, abilities, interests, and goals could lead to increased student satisfaction, academic achievement, and personal growth. The theoretical and research literature reviewed in this chapter will assist enrollment managers in the retention effort by providing a frame of reference not only for attracting students who will most likely be compatible with the institution, but also for managing the campus environment in order to provide an optimal educational experience for students.

Specifically, the chapter clarifies the concept of student-institution fit in the higher education setting and reviews important research findings that link degree of fit to student satisfaction and academic achievement. Perhaps more important, the chapter provides enrollment managers with a theory base on which the concept of student-institution fit is built. This theoretical foundation is important to an understanding of how students interact with their environments. Finally, the chapter discusses a systematic approach that can be followed to optimize levels of student-institution fit through environmental redesign. This approach includes conceptualizing the campus environment, assessing student-environment interaction, and then intervening in the environment to optimize the fit between students and their campus.

## Clarification of Student-Institution Fit

As enrollment managers define for their own institutions the nature of student-institution fit, they must carefully consider three important factors: student characteristics, institutional characteristics, and effects of the interaction between the student and the institution. Student characteristics include those personal attributes, needs, abilities, goals, expectations, interests, and values that students bring with them to the campus. Institutional characteristics include a complex array of physical, academic, social, and even psychological attributes that make up the campus environment, or climate of learning. Finally, the physical, cognitive, and affective interactions between students and their college or university constitute an important relationship that can lead to varying degrees of student satisfaction, academic achievement, and persistence in the institution. When students' needs, goals, and interests are adequately met by various environmental conditions and when student academic and social abilities mesh well with institutional requirements, then fit, or match, between student and institution is believed to exist.

Several authors have written about the concept of matching students with institutions of higher education in an effort to sensitize institutional leaders to issues surrounding student-institution fit. For example, Creager (1968) discusses fit by stating that the principal objective of matching students with colleges is to maximize educational objectives related to student persistence in college, motivation for gradute school, realistic career choice, high academic performance, certain values, and even mental health (p. 312). Painter and Painter (1982) believe that "the right choice will match the student with the college that fits personal abilities and personality, with understandable consequences of feelings of gratification. The wrong choice will cause frustration and angry blame-fixing by the student and college" (p. 86). Finally, Pace (1980) provides generalizations that are especially helpful to an understanding of student-institution fit: (1) Students entering college with highly unrealistic expectations about the environment are most likely to have problems adjusting and more likely to withdraw than are students who enter with realistic goals and expectations. (2) Students who perceive their campus environment to be friendly, congenial, and supportive are more likely to be satisfied with the college. (3) Student interaction with the scholastic press of the institution is directly related to goals for graduate study. (4) When congruency (or fit) exists between student personality characteristics and institutional characteristics, student objectives are more likely to be achieved (pp. 91–92).

## Outcomes of Student-Institution Fit

To appreciate what constitutes either optimal or poor fit between the student and the institution, one must examine the concepts of congruency and dissonance. A large number of studies have been conducted over the past 30 years specifically focused on the interaction between campus environments and students. For example, as early as 1963 Landis found that students who reported personal needs at variance with the campus environment were significantly less satisfied and withdrew in greater numbers than did students whose needs were more compatible with the campus press. In 1966 Lauterbach and Vielhaber found that congruency between student expectations for the college environment and perceived environmental press strongly influences student adjustment to the campus, thus leading to greater academic achievement. Brown (1968) found that the numerical dominance of a particular academic major on the campus did exert a significant impact on student feelings about college major, college satisfaction, and even social interaction. Morrow (1971) and Nafziger et al. (1975) also discovered that congruency between personality type, as measured by Holland's Vocational Preference Inventory, and college major led to significantly greater student satisfaction. Other studies have also compared student-institution fit with student satisfaction and achievement and have obtained similar findings (Pervin 1967; Walsh and Russell 1969; Starr, Betz, and Menne 1972).

Even though research results have both supported and rejected the basic congruency hypotheses regarding the relationship between fit and student satisfaction and achievement on the campus, there is agreement among many scholars that the research in general does support the link between fit and increased levels of student satisfaction with the institution, greater academic achievement, and enhanced personal growth (Walsh 1978; Huebner 1980; Lenning, Beal, and Sauer 1980).

## PERSON-ENVIRONMENT INTERACTION: A THEORY BASE

Student-institution fit in higher education is directly related to the broader theoretical concept of person-environment interaction. The importance in understanding factors contributing to person-environment interaction in higher education becomes very clear if one assumes that all aspects of human behavior—what one knows, feels, and does—cannot occur in a vacuum. Not only do people bring their own physical, social, and psychological characteristics into the environment, but the environment in which they live will necessarily have impact and influence on their behavior. Thus, the interactionist perspective would suggest that both the individual and the environment shape each other.

For college and university enrollment managers to be fully appreciative of, and sensitive to, factors influencing student-institution fit, they must be familiar with the theoretical foundation on which the concept of student-institution fit is established. This foundation consists of a family of theories that should be an integral part of the professional preparation of those seeking to be actively involved in enrollment planning and management in higher education.

Even though the concept of person-environment interaction in higher education has recently been the focus of much attention in the professional literature, the concept itself is not new. Theorists and researchers, especially from psychology and sociology dating back to 1924, have explored the relationships between individuals and their environments. Kantor (1924), Lewin (1936), and Murray (1938) each contributed to the theoretical foundation for interactionism. Over the past six decades, however, there has not been a consensus among theorists regarding the specific relationship between either personal characteristics, environmental characteristics, or their interaction on human behavior. In fact, over the years three basic theoretical approaches to explaining human behavior have been established. Ekehammer (1974) describes these approaches as personologism, situationism, and interactionism. *Personologism* describes behavior in terms of individual attributes or traits that cause people to behave in consistent ways across situations or environments. Thus, behavior is viewed as primarily internally directed. *Situationism* contends that behavior is externally controlled by the environment (or situation). Thus, one's behavior would change from setting to setting and personal characteristics would have little or no impact. *Interactionism* stresses that both the person and the environment interact and thus contribute to behavior. This position rejects personologism and situationism as sole determinants of behavior. It is this interactionist perspective that serves as the link between enrollment managers and their understanding of student-institution fit.

Walsh (1973, 1975, 1978) and Huebner (1980) provide excellent reviews and critiques of selected theories of person-environment interaction. Walsh reviewed several theoretical approaches that hold particular meaning for higher education: (1) Barker's (1968) theory of behavior settings; (2) Clark and Trow's (1966) subculture approach; (3) Holland's (1973) theory of personality; (4) Moos's (1973) social climate approach; and (5) Pervin's (1968) transactional approach. These theoretical approaches will be outlined briefly in the next section. The reader is advised, however, to turn to each theorist's original writings to gain a fuller understanding of the theoretical concepts.

## The Behavior-Setting Theory

Barker (1968) believes that both the individual and the environment must be considered in predicting behavior. However, his theory places more emphasis on the role of the environment than on the individual. The theory states that behavior settings (that is, a classroom, an athletic event, a library, or a concert) select and shape student behavior, and that regardless of individual differences among students, they tend to behave in very similar ways in specific environments. Thus, according to the theory, environments have a *coercive* influence on behavior.

According to this theory, there is an important link between the number of students in the campus environment who are available to perform essential functions of that setting and "the frequency, intensity, origin, and termination of forces that impinge upon these people" (Walsh 1978, p. 7). This means that students in campus environments without an adequate number of students available to support the environment's functions may feel threatened by the possibility of losing the satisfiers usually provided by the setting. Therefore, the individuals will become more involved in a greater variety of activities in order to maintain that setting. Thus, "people tend to be busier, more vigorous and more versatile" (Walsh 1978, p. 7). Research by both Barker (1968) and Walsh (1973) tends to support this concept by revealing that people in "undermanned" behavior settings tend to be personally more productive, involved, and satisfied than people in large settings.

Barker's interactionist approach has direct application to higher education. According to Walsh (1978), the theory suggests that student satisfaction and achievement may be functions of institutional size. Small colleges with underpopulated environments tend to provide students with more and diversified opportunities to experience and explore their interests and abilities. In the large institution, where there may be too many students for the number of functions operating within the settings (for example, opportunities for leadership), the opposite will occur. Barker and Gump (1964) refer to this as "redundancy." This occurs when the number of persons for a given setting exceeds the opportunities for active participation and satisfying experiences. Chickering (1969) has also linked the concept of redundancy to the affective development of individual students in the college environment. He states that "as redundancy sets in, the activities and responsibilities of those who do participate become more specialized and those with marginal qualifications are more quickly and more completely left out" (p. 147).

This theory suggests that enrollment managers carefully assess student behaviors and the environmental conditions on the campus that tend to shape or define those behaviors. In other words, a systematic examination of campus conditions that reinforce and thus shape student behavior both in and outside the classroom should be undertaken. In addition, the theory suggests that institutional leaders on large campuses attempt to identify or establish various subenvironments, or subcultures, that will reduce redundancy levels.

## The Subculture Approach

As with the behavior-setting theory, the subculture approach also focuses on the environment and the ways in which it influences and shapes the behavior of its inhabitants. Subcultures are essentially large behavior settings distinguished by the common characteristics (that is, attitudes and behaviors) of those who inhabit them. The basic theoretical assumption here is that individuals associated with a subculture interact and evidence common characteristics and behavior (Walsh 1978). This approach to person-environment interaction also assumes that people who compose a subculture are attracted to one another and are aware of their common interests and attitudes.

Walsh (1978) identifies several subculture models for student groups in higher education (see Bolton and Kammeyer 1967; Coleman 1966; Keniston 1966; Mauss 1967; Pemberton 1963; Schumer and Stanfield 1966; and Warren 1968). However, the subculture model of Clark and Trow (1966) is probably most commonly recognized because of its similarity to most of the other models.

Clark and Trow identified four types of campus subcultures: (1) collegiate, (2) vocational, (3) academic, and (4) nonconformist. Each subculture was devised from a combination of two variables: the degree to which students are involved with ideas and the extent to which students identify with their college.

1. The collegiate subculture is identified by strong student loyalty and attachment to the institution and little involvement with ideas and

academic issues over and above those required to graduate. This is a culture of "football, fraternities and sororities, dates, cars, drinking, and campus fun" (p. 20).

2. Students identifying with the vocational subculture have little attachment or loyalty to the college and are also resistant to intellectual demands beyond what are required of them to graduate. These students view higher education as "off-the-job training" and a series of courses leading only to a better job (p. 21).

3. The academic subculture is identified by students who work hard in their coursework, get the best grades, and actively pursue knowledge. These students also have a strong attachment to the institution, especially one that places much value on scholarship. Students identify closely with faculty and often aspire to graduate and professional schools (p. 22).

4. The nonconformist subculture is composed of students having much involvement with the world of ideas and little attachment to the institution itself. These students are very involved with ideas they encounter not only in their classes but also in the wider society. They maintain a critical detachment from the institution and its faculty and staff. Usually the student linked to this subculture is somewhat rebellious and is seeking a distinctive identity (p. 23).

Clark and Trow caution that the four categories are types of subcultures and not types of students, although these subcultures are often described by characterizing their student members. They also found that the individual student may well participate in more than one subculture on the campus, although usually one subculture will identify a student's major orientation.

Enrollment managers applying the subculture approach in their retention planning would need to define existing subcultures on the campus. It may well be that selected subculture typologies other than those identified by Clark and Trow may be more suitable for consideration. Once student subcultures have been identified, these data should be shared with prospective students to provide them with accurate information about peer group characteristics at the institution. According to Walsh (1978), subcultures may provide needed support for students by providing reinforcement of their attitudes, values, and behaviors, thus motivating them to enter and remain in the campus environments.

## The Personality Theory of John Holland

A third approach to person-environment interaction includes the extensive research that Holland (1973) has conducted in linking personality and environmental characteristics. Huebner (1980) identifies four major assumptions that Holland used in developing his theory:

1. People may be described by their resemblance to one or more personality types (or clusters of personal attributes). The six basic types, corresponding to vocational choice, are realistic, investigative, social, conventional, enterprising, and artistic.
2. Environments may also be described by their resemblance to one or more of six model environments. These environments correspond to the six personality types.
3. Each personality type searches for an analogous environment.
4. Congruent person-environment relationships lead to predictable and understandable outcomes with respect to vocational choice, stability, and achievement; personal stability and development; and creative performance. (p. 126)

Since Holland believed that behavior is a function of both personality and environment, he was concerned about the level of fit, or congruence, between the person and the environment. He created a hexagonal model on which personality or environmental types were fixed as a result of their correlational relationships with each other. In other words, those personality or environmental types that were found to be statistically similar to one another (for example, enterprising and conventional) were placed closest together on the hexagon. According to Walsh (1978), over 150 research studies have been conducted using Holland's theory. He reports that the research supports the existence of a link between personality types and environmental models. Further, the evidence indicates that people tend to select college environments and occupational environments consistent with their personality types. Finally, the research also supports Holland's fourth assumption that congruent person-environment interactions are associated with personal and vocational stability and satisfaction (p. 9). Thus, Holland's interactionism approach can have significant meaning for enrollment managers in the higher education setting. The research underscores the value of assisting students to understand more clearly the relationships between their own personality characteristics and broad vocational preferences before making a final decision to attend a particular institution. Institutions might consider conducting self-studies to determine whether one or more model environments exist on the campus. This information could be shared with prospective students via college admissions counselors, through high school counselors, and in printed brochures and college bulletins.

## The Social Ecological Approach

Rudolph Moos (1974) promotes the concept that environments, like people, also have unique personalities, and thus it is possible to describe an environment as one would describe an individual's personality. His approach is based on the writings of Lewin (1936), Murray (1938), and Stern (1964, 1970). Moos's approach assumes that social environments can be described as they are perceived by their inhabitants. Thus, people would describe the usual patterns of behavior that occur in their setting plus their own perceptions of the environment. Perhaps most important, Moos also assumes that the way individuals perceive their environment directly influences their behavior.

Moos studied eight different types of social environments and found that three common dimensions exist across environments. First, there is a *relationship* dimension, which consists of the extent to which people are involved in the environment and the extent to which they support one another. Specific relationship factors include involvement, affiliation, staff support, peer cohesion, and spontaneity. The second dimension is made up of *personal development* factors, which include opportunities in the environment for personal growth and development of self-esteem. The third common dimension includes *system maintenance* and *change*. This dimension consists of the extent to which the environment is orderly, clear in its expectations, and responsive to change (Walsh 1978). Moos concluded that all three dimensions are necessary for understanding the social environment.

Moos and his colleagues developed several perceptual climate scales for measuring psychosocial environmental characteristics. Specifically, groups of scales were developed for four different types of environments: (1) treatment environments (Ward Atmosphere Scale, Moos 1976d; Community-Oriented Programs Environment Scale, Moos 1976a); (2) institutional environments (Correctional Institutions Environment Scale, Moos 1976b); (3) educational environments (University Residence Environment Scale, Moos and Gerst 1976; Classroom Environment Scale, Moos and Trickett 1976); and (4) community environments (Work Environment Scale, Moos and Insel 1976; Group Environment Scale, Moos and Humphrey 1976; Family Environment Scale, Moos 1976c).

In suggesting implications for higher education, Walsh (1978) indicates that Moos's social climate scales can be helpful in understanding the college and university environment—its effects on inhabitants and how responsive it might be to change (p. 13). He reports that Insel and Moos (1974) have found "the climate of environments in which people live and function influences their satisfaction, self-esteem, and personal development" (Walsh 1978, p. 14). Further evidence also suggests that the perceived social environment can have important physiological and health-related effects (p. 14).

Enrollment managers using Moos's approach may examine factors within the campus social environment along the relationship, personal development, and system maintenance and change dimensions. It is critical in this examination to collect student, faculty, and staff perceptions of the social environment and to determine their relationship to behavior.

## The Person-Environment Transactional Approach

Pervin (1968) proposes that behavior results from interactions between the person and the environment. He believes environments exist for each person that tend to match the individual's perception of self. Thus, when individuals are in environments congruent with their self-perceived personality characteristics, higher performance, greater satisfaction, and reduced discomfort and stress will occur. Pervin bases his approach on certain assumptions: first, that individuals find major discrepancies between their perceived actual and ideal selves to be unpleasant and painful, and second, that people are positively attracted to environments that can move them toward their ideal selves. Conversely, individuals are negatively disposed toward environmental factors that move them away from their ideal selves (Walsh 1978, p. 12).

Pervin (1967) uses the Transactional Analysis of Personality and Environment (TAPE) to measure self-reported perceptions of both person and environment. Walsh (1978) reports that limited research tentatively suggests that self-environment similarity tends to be associated with greater self-reported satisfaction in college environments. This finding, according to Walsh, is consistent with research using both Holland's and the subculture approach to interactionism. Thus, Pervin's approach suggests that enrollment managers assist students in assessing their perceptions of their actual and ideal selves as well as their perceptions of the campus environment. An important role, then, for enrollment managers is to describe to students the potential of the campus environment for facilitating movement (personal growth) toward their ideal selves. The environmental assessment undertaken may also reveal that the campus environment does not hold that potential for a significant number of currently enrolled students. At this point enrollment managers must determine in what ways to modify or redesign the environment in order to facilitate student growth and development.

## A Congruency Model

Cope and Hannah (1975) also believe that in higher education a direct link exists between student-institution fit and retention. Their research revealed that the lack of congruency between student and institution accounted for most of student transferring, stopping out, and dropping out (p. 3). They describe five factors where incongruency between student and college can lead to attrition: poor college choice, institutional bureaucracy, quality of instruction, search for identity, and value confrontations.

Specifically, they state that a large percentage of students transfer from their first college simply because they made a poor assessment of the social and intellectual climate of the institution. What they expect to find just does not materialize. Thus, they feel they made a poor choice. Institutional bureaucracy in combination with other factors, especially in the large university, may cause students to develop negative attitudes toward persistence. The researchers found that "dealing with the bureaucracy becomes one more 'cost' to consider against the benefit of the degree or of learning something" (p. 34). They also report that quality of teaching, size of classes, and reliance on lecturing were related to attrition, again in the large university. Additionally, students who experience major identity crises usually become stopouts or dropouts. For example, Cope and Hannah report that students in crisis will say they are leaving the college "to find myself, to discover what kind of person I really want to be, to have an opportunity to think through what I really believe, and so forth" (p. 35). Finally, they found that value conflicts among students and between students and their college environment lead to self-doubt, defensiveness, and possible reevaluation of the student's place in the environment. Areas of value conflict usually include religion, morality-sexuality standards, and politics and usually occur during the first year in college (p. 37).

## Summary

The first five theoretical approaches to person-environment interaction all stress to varying degrees that human behavior is a function of characteristics of the person in interaction with the environment. Each theorist, however, conceptualizes person-environment interaction and its effect on behavior in different ways.

Three of the theorists emphasize the effect of the environment on behavior almost to the exclusion of the person. Barker (1968) stresses that behavior settings shape human behavior and that regardless of individual differences, people behave in similar ways in specific environments. Clark and Trow (1966) in their subculture approach also focus on the college environment and the ways in which it influences and shapes student be-havior. Moos's social ecological approach (1974) also concentrates primarily on the social climate of environments and the effects social characteristics have on human behavior.

The remaining two theorists tend to focus primarily on the role of the individual in person-environment interactionism. Holland (1973), when utilizing his hexagonal model, emphasizes the personality characteristics of the individual. He applied the same personality characteristics to environ-mental structures, thus creating six model environments compatible with the hexagonal personality model. Pervin's (1968) transactional approach also stresses the self-perceptions of the individual, thus focusing more on the individual than on the environment.

Chapter 6, which discusses student retention research, reviews two ad-ditional theoretical approaches that have recently been developed regarding the relationship between student-institution fit and student retention in higher education (Tinto 1975; Bean 1983). Enrollment managers should also become familiar with these theoretical perspectives if they are to understand and appreciate more fully the role of the institutional environ-ment in student attrition and retention.

## OPTIMIZING STUDENT-INSTITUTION FIT THROUGH CAMPUS REDESIGN

This chapter has clarified the concept of student-institution fit and its link to student retention in terms of the interactions between student inputs and institutional inputs. It has also been shown that a comprehensive theoretical foundation related to person-environment interaction can pro-vide the enrollment manager with a variety of ways to understand how students and institutions interact with each other. The research reveals that congruency, or fit, between students and their campus environments is important and leads to student satisfaction and achievement. What remains to be discussed is how those responsible for enrollment management in higher education can translate the theoretical concepts and research find-ings into effective student retention plans.

The remainder of this chapter describes three major tasks that enroll-ment managers and their institutional colleagues should undertake to op-timize the fit between students and their institution: (1) Conceptualize the campus environment—that is, how will the campus environment be char-acterized, described, defined? (2) Assess the campus environment—that is, how and with what assessment tools will the environment be measured? (3) Intervene in the campus environment to optimize student-institution fit and thus retention—that is, what changes might be made in the environment that will result in higher levels of congruency between the environment and the students?

## Conceptualizing Campus Environments

Banning and McKinley (1980) provide an excellent review of several ways to conceptualize campus environments. To understand the nature of student-institution fit on any given campus, enrollment managers must have a comprehensive understanding of their own campus environment, or climate of learning, before they can begin to assess the impact it has on students. Selected approaches for conceptualizing campus environments reviewed here include those of Moos (1974), Blocher (1974, 1978), and Astin (1968).

*Moos's classification system.* Moos (1974) proposes a six-part classification system for studying human environments, which can also be applied to higher education. Each of the six dimensions in the system would be specifically examined in the campus environment for its effect on students. The dimensions are the following: (1) *Geographic, meteorological, architectural, and physical design* dimensions are all important and often overlooked factors that can affect the relationship between student and institution. For example, the geographic location of the campus in combination with weather conditions can affect student comfort levels in academic buildings and residence units. The age of campus buildings and their location (especially on the large university campus) can also affect student attitudes and behavior—for example, course enrollments. (2) *Behavior settings* in the campus environment shape student behavior regardless of student personality (see Barker 1968). For example, classrooms, residence hall rooms, student government meetings, and athletic events are all examples of behavior settings. Each setting affects student behavior in different ways. (3) *Organizational structures* in the environment can also affect students. For example, levels of institutional bureaucracy students perceive can affect their attitudes toward the institution. Also, as student government becomes more organized and centralized, it may have a more powerful impact on the institution, affecting such matters as campus issues, funded activities, and relationships among students and faculty and administration. (4) *Personal and behavioral characteristics* of students, faculty, and staff who constitute the campus environment can be potent factors in the environment. These characteristics compose the social climate of the campus and can affect students in many different ways. For example, groups of students, especially minorities, may note that their peer group is generally of a different race, religion, ethnic background, or even age; as a result, they can become uncomfortable, lonely, or alienated in the environment. (5) *Organizational climate and psychosocial characteristics* are the fifth dimension, for which Moos draws on the writings of Chickering (1969) and Pervin (1968). Chickering found that as the clarity and consistency of institutional objectives (a measure of organizational climate) increase, student development in such areas as personal competence, autonomy, and purpose is fostered. Pervin has proposed that campus environments can be described by student perceptions of the psychosocial characteristics of the environment. When student perception of the campus matches self-perception, higher performance and satisfaction will result. (6) *Systematic analysis of reinforcers in the environment* arises from the assumption that behavior results from the reinforcement consequences associated with the behavior. Thus, the campus should be carefully and systematically examined to detect the ways in which student behavior (both positive and negative) is being reinforced by the environment.

Moos's approach for conceptualizing campus environments provides a comprehensive scheme that can be quite useful to enrollment managers. Several of the person-environment interaction theories described earlier have been incorporated. This is but one approach; there are others.

*Blocher's environmental subsystems.* A second way to conceptualize campus environments includes the work of Blocher (1974, 1978), who describes three subsystems or structures for analyzing any given environment. Each subsystem includes two or more environmental conditions. The first subsystem is the *opportunity structure,* which identifies opportunities in the environment for student involvement in a variety of experiences, opportunities for challenging experiences that lead to intrinsic rewards for students, and opportunities for the student to integrate experience in the environment in a safe, reflective, and unhurried atmosphere. Thus, in this first subsystem the three key conditions are involvement, challenge, and integration.

The second subsystem is the *support structure,* which consists of environmental resources available to the student for dealing with stress. These resources include networks of positive human relationships (a support condition) and performance models slightly more advanced than current levels of student performance. These models (faculty, staff, and peers in roles as paraprofessionals) are important in that students must see that environmental tasks can be mastered.

The third subsystem is the *reward structure,* which offers the environmental conditions of feedback and application. Feedback occurs when the student receives clear, accurate, and immediate information about performance relative to environmental demands. The application condition exists if students have a variety of opportunities to actively apply new concepts, attitudes, and skills in the environment.

Banning (1980) has developed a Management Template for Campus Ecology, using Blocher's dimensions of opportunity, support, and reward. The template can serve as an effective tool for conceptualizing campus environments.

*Astin's concept of the campus environment.* Astin (1968), in his major research on the college environment, developed the Inventory of College Activities (ICA) to measure stimuli in the college environment, the college image, and student characteristics. His conceptualization of the college environment centered around four factors: (1) peer environment, (2) classroom environment, (3) administrative environment, and (4) physical environment. The *peer environment,* in part, included the following factors: competitiveness versus cooperativeness, organized dating, independence, cohesiveness, leisure time, career indecision, library use, and employment. The *classroom environment* included class involvement, verbal aggressiveness, instructor extraversion, student familiarity with instructor, classroom organization, and grading severity. The *administrative environment* included the severity of policies against drinking, aggression, heterosexual activity, and cheating. The *physical environment* included such factors as spread of the campus, physical climate, and characteristics of living units (p. 119).

Even though the three approaches described above are not an exhaustive coverage of ways to conceptualize campus environments, they are a good representative sample of available approaches. It may well be that enrollment managers will wish to refine their own conceptualizations by drawing on parts of these approaches to form a new approach tailored to the uniqueness of their own campuses.

## Assessing Campus Environments

Once enrollment managers determine how to conceptualize their campus environments, they next need to devise a plan for the systematic assessment of all aspects of the environment and its interaction effects with students. Huebner (1980) critiques four measures that can be used to conduct person-environment assessment: demographic, perceptual, behavioral, and multimethod approaches. She reports that the *demographic* method is primarily descriptive and is concerned with variables such as institutional size, student ability levels, faculty size, student-faculty ratio, and size of library holdings. Instruments such as the Environmental Assessment Technique

(EAT) by Astin and Holland (1961) and Holland's (1971) Self-Directed Search (SDS) are examples of demographic assessment tools. Huebner reports that even though the demographic approach has advantages, this approach "appears to be most useful in providing data to augment and clarify results from other types of assessment" (p. 135).

The *perceptual* approach to assessment is the best developed and most widely used and allows institutions to collect and compare perceptual data from all campus constituencies. Well-known instruments in this category include the Transactional Analysis of Personality and Environment (TAPE) (Pervin 1967); the Classroom Environment Scale (Moos and Trickett 1976); the University Residence Environment Scale (URES) (Moos and Gerst 1976); the College Characteristics Index (CCI) (Pace and Stern 1958); the Organizational Climate Index (Stern 1970); the Activities Index (AI) (Pace and Stern 1958); the College and University Environment Scales (CUES) (Pace 1969); and the Institutional Goals Inventory (Educational Testing Service 1972). Huebner (1980) reports the advantages of the perceptual approach include its "sensitivity to person-environment change, straightforward interpretation, less need for representative sampling (from Centra 1970), and the availability of several published, psychometrically adequate instruments" (pp. 135–136). Morrill (1973), Centra (1968), and Jackson and Levine (1977) also suggest limitations to the use of perceptual instruments.

The *behavioral* approach utilizes assessment instruments that measure specific, observable behaviors of students, faculty, and staff. Huebner states that this approach is the least developed among the four methods, but some measures are available. For example, the Experience of College Questionnaire (ECQ) (McDowell and Chickering 1967) and Astin's (1971) Inventory of College Activities (ICA) would be included in this category. She adds that this approach can provide both accurate and detailed accounts of activities within a campus environment, which can pinpoint specific campus issues that other assessment approaches may overlook.

The fourth measure in person-environment assessment is the *multimethod* approach, which combines demographic, perceptual, and behavioral approaches in an effort to collect a wide variety of data in a single assessment. Huebner identifies two instruments that would be included in this category: Peterson's (1968) College Student Questionnaire (CSQ) and Centra's (1970) Questionnaire on Student and College Characteristics.

Huebner concludes her critique with five recommendations: (1) Environments need not be viewed as monolithic; rather, subenvironments should be identified and studied independently in relation to each other. (2) Descriptive instruments designed for interinstitutional comparisons are inadequate for assessment of a single institution. (3) Locally designed assessment tools may be more useful than standardized instruments in planning environmental intervention. (4) Multiple approaches to assessment should be used to achieve a fuller understanding of environments and person-environment relationships. (5) Relationships between "objective" and "perceived" environments should be further defined (p. 137).

Pace (1980) also provides useful guidelines for developing diagnostic instruments for environmental assessment. Those responsible for enrollment management should carefully consider these guidelines when selecting or designing assessment instruments. He suggests that measures of college environments should (1) characterize the environment along four or five major dimensions; (2) have an explicit content structure so that different segments of the environment or sources of press can be identified; and (3) characterize the environment at two levels—collegewide and sub-environment levels (p. 106).

Several sources in the literature can provide valuable assistance to enrollment managers seeking more information about assessment of person-environment interaction. The reader should review Baird and Hartnett (1980), especially the chapter by Pace on "Assessing Diversity among Campus Groups" and the final chapter, which provides an annotated directory of 20 leading instruments for assessing campus environments. Aulepp and Delworth (1978) also provide an informative overview of how to devise various environmental assessment techniques.

## Intervening for Environmental Redesign

There is growing recognition among faculty and especially student affairs professionals in higher education that campus environments and students need to be "fitted" together more carefully, that the appropriate and responsible use of the campus environment by students should be systematically facilitated, that increased accuracy and speed of communication between students and their environment should occur, and that both students and their environments should be more responsive to each other's needs, requirements, and structures (Huebner 1980, p. 139). To effectively respond to these concerns, enrollment managers must devise interventions that focus on the important issues related to student-institution fit. This will require a focus not only on the student but also on the campus environment and the interaction between the two.

Banning and McKinley (1980) suggest that students in the higher education setting who experience a "mismatch," resulting in academic, social, or personal adjustment problems, have traditionally been viewed as deficient in some manner. This perspective has evolved from an institutional reliance on a counseling and medical model in which students are seen as clients. This approach has, until recently, turned attention away from the campus environment and the transactional relationship between students and their environment. When students are viewed as clients, campus environments are rarely seen as "ill" or in need of intervention (p. 40). Banning and Kaiser (1974) add that if institutions always assume that students are deficient in some way, institutional efforts may at times be aimed at helping the student adjust or accommodate to a deficient campus environment (see also Banning 1980, pp. 209–212).

Since 1975 only a few intervention models have been developed that view the student, the campus environment, and the student-environment interaction as integral parts of an intervention process. Two of these models will be reviewed next: the Ecosystem Model and the Ecomapping Model.

*The Ecosystem Model.* Also known as the Ecosystem Design Process, the Ecosystem Model (Kaiser 1975) was conceptualized after several basic assumptions were made (Kaiser 1978, p. 26):

1.  Campus environments consist of all physical, chemical, biological, and social stimuli that impinge on students.
2.  Students shape their environment and at the same time are shaped by it—a truly transactional relationship.
3.  Campus environments may facilitate or inhibit a wide spectrum of student behavior.
4.  Students will attempt to cope with any campus environment in which they are placed.
5.  Because of individual differences among students, a variety of campus subenvironments should be designed.
6.  Successful environmental design is dependent on full participation of all campus constituencies.

The Ecosystem Model consists of seven basic stages: (1) Several environmental values considered desirable for the campus environment are selected through consensus exercises such as values clarification. All campus constituencies are involved. (2) The list of environmental values is prioritized and a few are selected for translation into measurable, programmatic goal statements. (3) Goal statements are translated into observable and tangible student programs and activities. (4) Programs and activities in the campus environment are fitted to meet the needs of students. These needs may require special programs at the macrolevel (campuswide), microlevel (selected groups), or life-space level (for the individual). (5) Student perceptions of the campus environment are measured (using a variety of instruments) and compared with goal statements established in stage 2 above. A special focus is placed on stimuli or referents in the environment that evoke the measured perceptions. These referents could include students, faculty, staff, policies, curriculums, and physical facilities. (6) Student behavior on the campus is observed, measured, and compared with perceptions identified in stage 5. If the ecosystem design is working, a high correspondence between behavior (stage 6), perceptions (stage 5), and goals (stage 2) should exist. (7) The final stage consists of a recycling of all the data collected in stages 1 to 6 back to stage 1 for further review and perhaps clarification of environmental values previously identified. At this point the ecosystem design process begins again.

Kaiser (1978) reports that several campuses have used the Ecosystem Model in designing environmental interventions. In fact, a training manual has been prepared to assist campus personnel with the design (see Aulepp and Delworth 1976). This comprehensive process for intervening in the campus environment is truly an interactionist perspective, which takes into account both the student and the environment and their interaction. The complexity of the design, however, mandates that all campus constituencies be integrally involved, and thus the model requires full support from the highest levels of the institution.

*The Ecomapping Model.* An alternative approach to the design of person-environment interventions on the campus is the Ecomapping Model (Huebner and Corrazzini 1976). This model was developed in the belief that resources in the campus environment are expected to meet student needs. The students, to fulfill their needs, engage in a "mapping" process, which requires them to identify and use various resources available in the campus environment. The degree to which there is fit between the students' needs and their successful identification and utilization of resources determines congruence.

The Ecomapping Model is composed of a ten-step process that takes into consideration both the individual and the campus environment. The process includes the following: step 1—establish a campus-based design team (faculty, staff, and students); step 2—assess perceived and actual environmental features; step 3—conduct needs assessment for subgroups on the campus (for example, subgroups of students) and assess student perceptions of the degree to which needs are met; step 4—examine matches and mismatches between perceived environmental features and student needs; step 5—compare matches and mismatches with the actual environment; step 6—assess how students have coped with various mismatches (that is, unmet needs); step 7—have design team collect all assessment data from steps 2 to 6; step 8—have design team analyze data and determine what changes in the environment should be made; step 9—have design team plan and carry out specific activities to incorporate the needed changes; step 10—reassess to evaluate whether the degree of mismatch between students and their campus environment has been reduced.

Huebner and Corrazzini (1976) suggest that campus personnel responsible for implementing the Ecomapping Model use a variety of assessment methods (questionnaire, interview, observation) and assessment foci (perceptions, behaviors, events, demographics) in order to receive a fuller description of the campus environment.

The two intervention models reviewed provide the enrollment management team on the campus with detailed processes for minimizing mismatches between students and institutions. Because the examples provided are models, they do not promote any particular person-environment interaction theory. As was pointed out earlier, enrollment managers can choose from diverse theoretical frameworks that can be applied to whichever model is selected.

## LINKING ENROLLMENT MANAGEMENT AND STUDENT-INSTITUTION FIT

The purpose of this chapter has been to introduce and clarify for enrollment managers in higher education important concepts linking student-institution fit and student retention. It has been shown that a comprehensive research-and-theory base exists for understanding the complex ways in which students interact with their institutions. This research reveals that congruency, or fit, between students and their campuses results in increased satisfaction, achievement, and retention. Enrollment managers must recognize the need to design retention programs that consider not only the student characteristics but also those of the institutional environment. This concern for the interaction between student and institution requires campus leaders to conceptualize and assess the various components of the institutional environment and then to carefully design interventions that will make the fit between students and campus most effective. This process thus requires that enrollment managers develop a systematic approach to environmental evaluation and that they are prepared to alter the campus environment whenever necessary. This growing body of knowledge is yet another content area with which the emerging profession of enrollment managers must become familiar if they are to plan and manage their campus enrollments effectively.

## SUGGESTIONS FOR FURTHER READING

*Campus Ecology: A Perspective for Student Affairs,* by James H. Banning.
"Conceptions of the Campus Environment," by James H. Banning and D. L. McKinley. In W. H. Morrill, J. C. Hurst, and E. R. Oetting (eds.), *Dimensions of Intervention for Student Development.*
"Assessing Diversity among Campus Groups," by C. R. Pace. In L. L. Baird, R. T. Hartnett, and Associates (eds.), *Understanding Student and Faculty Life.*
"Placing Students for Stability and Success," by P. Painter and N. Painter. In W. R. Lowery and Associates (eds.), *College Admissions Counseling.*
*Theories of Person-Environment Interaction: Implications for the College Student,* by W. B. Walsh.

# Chapter 6

# Retaining Students

## AN OVERVIEW

Although the concept of enrollment management is new, concern for student retention is not. The first major study on student attrition was done for the U.S. Department of Education on the entering classes of 1931 and 1932 (Ramist 1981). Later studies emerged in 1958 (Iffert) and 1962 (Summerskill). It was not until college enrollments began to level off in the 1970s, however, that college and university administrators became seriously concerned about this issue.

Research on college student attrition has now become familiar to many administrators and faculty within the United States higher education system. Few colleges and universities across the country have not investigated their own retention rates. Many institutions have attempted to implement campus-based programs to reduce student attrition.

Since the study of student attrition is not new to most enrollment managers, this chapter begins with a brief review of research and programs in student retention. This review examines the characteristics of students who withdraw and persist as well as programs developed to improve retention. The focus then shifts to the most promising new research developments on student persistence and the potential applications for enrollment managers. As will become evident, marketing and targeting retention programs, along with the careful evaluation of such efforts, may well be just as important in retaining students as it is in attracting them.

## RESEARCH ON STUDENT ATTRITION

Much of the research on student attrition has focused on the characteristics of those who dropped out of college before graduation. The assumption has been that if institutions of higher learning could identify the characteristics of students who withdraw, they would be able to develop programs to meet the needs of these students. The studies can be grouped into three major categories: student qualities at the time of matriculation, institutional traits or characteristics, and student experiences at the institution of attendance.

Student qualities at the time of matriculation can be broken down into the following subcategories:

1. Demographic factors—sex, race, family income level, parents' educational level, family encouragement, and residence characteristics.
2. Student personality factors, aspirations, and motivations—emotional stability, flexibility, maturity, educational and career aspirations, and motivation to continue education.
3. High school experience—involvement in high school activities, quality of high school, and so forth.

In addition to the characteristics of the student, institutions have traits or qualities that have been associated with student persistence:

4. Institutional size.
5. Type and control of institution—two-year or four-year, public or private, sectarian or nonsectarian.
6. Selectivity.
7. Coeducation.

The experiences of the student after matriculation can be divided into the subcategories listed below:

8. Academic factors—collegiate grade point average, academic program enrolled in.
9. Discovery of significant others—the establishment of close friendships and significant relationships on campus.
10. Involvement with the campus—the level of involvement in student activities and events, use of campus facilities and services.
11. College residence—living at home, in residence halls, in Greek housing, or in off-campus housing.
12. Financial assistance—the amount and type of financial assistance.

Most of the research on the characteristics of persisters and nonpersisters can be organized under these three major headings and twelve subgroupings.

## STUDENT QUALITIES AT MATRICULATION

### Demographic Factors

Some of the earliest studies on persistence examined the demographic characteristics of students who withdrew and those who graduated. This was a natural first step because college administrators wanted to know what persisters and nonpersisters "looked like." Most campus-based retention programs continue to monitor demographic data on their students. This is a relatively easy and potentially useful way to monitor their dropouts. Factors such as race, family income level, parents' educational level, and residence characteristics of persisters and withdrawers are typically tracked.

Research on persistence among men and women has revealed differences between the two sexes. According to Astin (1975), women are more likely than men to complete a baccalaureate degree in four years. Ramist (1981), however, notes that if college graduation rates are tracked over a 10-year period, men are more likely to graduate; there is a greater likelihood that women will leave school for voluntary reasons and men will leave for academic reasons. Hilton (1982), however, reports very little difference in the persistence rates of men and women. Lenning, Sauer, and Beal (1980a), conclude that when socioeconomic status, ability, and motivation are controlled, the sex of the student is unrelated to persistence.

Several studies demonstrate that minority students are more likely to drop out than are nonminority students (Astin 1975; Lenning, Sauer, and Beal 1980a; Pascarella et al. 1981; Ramist 1981). However, most of the differences between the retention rates of white and nonwhite students tend to disappear when the socioeconomic levels and ability levels of the students are controlled (Astin 1975; Hilton 1982; Ramist 1981). Astin reveals that black students are more likely to drop out of predominantly white colleges than predominantly black ones. He also notes that oriental students have lower rates of withdrawal than any other ethnic group.

Not surprisingly, an important demographic characteristic of students is their ability level. Since the true ability level of a student is seldom known in most retention studies, high school grade point average, class rank, and college entrance test scores are usuually used as indirect measures of ability. As these three indicators of a college matriculant's ability rise, so do the student's chances for graduation (Astin 1975; Bean 1980; Fetters 1977; Lenning, Sauer, and Beal 1980a,b; Pascarella et al. 1981; Ramist 1981; Spady 1970; Tinto 1975). High school grade point average and class rank are the two best predictors of persistence (Ramist 1981).

The income level of students' parents also appears to be related to persistence at first glance. When included in regression analysis along with parental level of education, student ability, and motivation, however, parental income level does not seem to exert an influence upon dropping out (Astin 1975; Pascarella et al. 1981). Although parental income level may not exert a direct influence on dropping out, Lenning, Sauer, and Beal (1980a) conclude that the income level of parents is important because it affects the precollege environment, student personality characteristics, motivation, and student ability.

Parental income levels have also been examined along with their educational background. Separate studies conducted by Astin (1975) and Fetters (1977) conclude that the educational level of parents is inversely related to student withdrawal from college before graduation. This proves to be a more influential variable than parental income level.

The level of family encouragement to pursue higher learning is also related to student attrition. As already stated, the level of parental income and the educational level of parents probably shape the precollege environment of students. Several studies document a positive relationship between student persistence and the level of parental encouragement (Hilton 1982; Lenning, Sauer, and Beal 1980a; Pantages and Creedon 1968; Tinto 1975). Astin's (1975) findings show that financial support from parents is also related to continuance. Parental financial support might be used as one more measure of parental encouragement.

Where a matriculating student resides also seems to make a difference in persistence rates. Students who live in rural areas and small towns have higher dropout rates than do students coming from urban and metropolitan areas (Astin 1975; Ramist 1981). Ramist also finds that out-of-state students attending institutions that are not contiguous to the state in which they reside have higher attrition rates than either out-of-state students from contiguous states or in-state students. Finally, students from the West and Southwest are more likely to drop out than are students from other geographical areas (Astin 1975). These results may be confounded by the fact that community colleges, which have the highest attrition rates of any type of institution, are a more dominant form of higher education in these regions.

## Student Personality Factors, Aspirations, and Motivation

The qualities that students bring with them to the college or university of their choice also affect their ability to persist until graduation. Their personality characteristics, their academic and career aspirations, as well as the importance of more schooling and their desire to graduate can all influence the likelihood of dropping out.

Lenning, Sauer, and Beal (1980a) note that the student's level of self-confidence and self-concept are correlated with persistence. The higher the level of self-esteem, the more likely the student is to graduate. Cope and Hannah (1975) and Pantages and Creedon (1968) describe some of the personality characteristics of dropouts. Although the descriptions are somewhat contradictory, certain qualities appear to be similar. Generally, withdrawing students, as opposed to continuing students, tend to be more critical, nonconforming, resentful of regulations, assertive of their individuality, and lacking in goal directedness.

With respect to academic and career aspirations, the differences between persisters and leavers are not contradictory. Plans to enter graduate school are closely tied to high retention. In fact, as the academic aspirations of students rise, their rate of persistence also rises (Astin 1975). Students who do not expect to earn a degree are the most likely to drop out (Ramist 1981). The impact of entering college undecided about vocational goals cannot be clearly determined at this point. In Ramist's excellent review of the literature on attrition, he cites research findings that suggest that being undecided can have a negative relationship to continuance. He also refers to studies that have found there is no relationship between these two variables.

The motivation of the student to attend and complete college is one of the best predictors of student retention. Student self-reports in areas such as the importance of earning a college degree, the importance attached to education, and the likelihood of transferring or dropping out are powerful indicators of persistence and withdrawal (Astin 1975; Bean 1980; Lenning, Sauer, and Beal 1980a, Pascarella et al. 1981; Terenzini et al. 1981; Ramist 1981). The best single method for predicting student attrition may simply be to ask students about their educational plans and the likelihood that they will graduate from the institution they are attending.

## School Experiences

The type of high school a student attends and the kinds of experiences a student has are also related to college persistence. Astin reports that matriculants who enter with better study habits are more likely to graduate. He also notes a positive relationship between the students' own rankings of high school quality and continuance. After looking at College Board data, Ramist states that the type of courses taken in high school affects dropout rates. Students who took more English, foreign languge, and mathematics courses in high school were more likely to graduate. Finally, Astin finds that students who receive a varsity letter in high school have lower withdrawal rates. He speculates that this may reflect the fact that such students are more likely to receive scholarships subsequently or that they are more predisposed to becoming involved in campus activities upon matriculation.

Although this section has examined the prematriculation traits of high school students, community college transfer students can be considered matriculants to four-year colleges and universities. There is a paucity of research in this area and more work is needed. The work of Newlon and Gaither (1980) at one large state university suggests that community college transfer students have lower retention rates than matriculants entering as freshmen. This is true even when background characteristics are controlled.

The authors speculate that this may be the result of inferior preparation, transfer of credit problems, or motivational problems (p. 242).

Each of these student characteristics contributes to student attrition. Retention problems, however, involve more than just student traits. There are also institutional traits that appear to be correlated with student attrition.

## INSTITUTIONAL CHARACTERISTICS

### Size

Ramist (1981), after reviewing the results of several studies, reports there is no clear evidence to support the belief that size has any effect on retention rates. In his 1977 work on the impact of college on students, Astin states that larger colleges reduce the opportunity for student involvement. However, there remains no clear pattern of student retention rates based on institutional size.

### Type and Control

Two-year colleges have considerably lower retention rates than do four-year institutions (Astin 1975, Deal and Noel 1980, Fetters 1977; Lenning, Sauer, and Beal 1980a; Ramist 1981)—perhaps because community colleges often have larger proportions of students with less ability, who come from lower socioeconomic levels. In addition, many community college students have less family experience with higher education and are less committed to graduating.

Most research suggests that private colleges have slightly better retention rates than do public institutions, even when the ability and socioeconomic background of the students are controlled. Astin suggests that these differences can be attributed to residence halls, more financial aid, and more on-campus work opportunities at private colleges.

Once again turning to Astin's work, some interesting results are reported. Catholic colleges appear to exert a strong holding power on their students; fewer than 25 percent of both male and female students drop out before graduating (p. 113). In comparison, among all private colleges as a group, 27 percent of their men and 24 percent of their women fail to persist (p. 113). Astin concludes that the slightly negative influence on retention rates evidenced by private colleges must be the result of reports from the nondenominational colleges (p. 114).

### Selectivity

Ramist (1981) reports that Admissions Testing Program–Summary Report Service (ATP-SRS) data collected by the College Board show that even when ability levels are controlled, students attending more selective colleges and universities have a greater chance of persisting. Astin's (1977) results support these findings. He also writes that attending more selective institutions does not increase the probability of dropping out, even when ability levels are held constant.

## Coeducation

Perhaps surprisingly, single-sex colleges hold their students better than do coeducational colleges. According to Astin the attrition rate at single-sex colleges for women is 23 percent versus 32 percent for women at coeducational institutions (p. 117). Similarly, the dropout rate at all-male colleges is 28 percent as opposed to 38 percent at coeducational schools (p. 117).

As this review has pointed out, there are certain institutional qualities that seem to be related to student persistence. The problem of student attrition, however, is complex and must also be viewed from the perspective of how the student interacts with the campus environment after matriculation.

## STUDENT EXPERIENCES IN COLLEGE

### Academic Factors

Astin (1975) notes a direct correlation between the grades of college students and their persistence rates. Practically every college student with a C− grade point average, or less, drops out, and students with a B average are almost twice as likely to drop out when compared with A students (p. 98). Bean (1983) and Ramist (1981) also found university grades to be an important variable in the ability to predict student withdrawal. Research conducted by Pascarella et al. (1981) also identifies college grades as a factor in student retention.

### Significant Others

The importance of having a significant relationship with at least one other person on campus has consistently been found to be related to student attrition (Astin 1975; Bean 1983; Lenning, Sauer, and Beal 1980a; Noel 1978; Ramist 1981; Terenzini and Pascarella 1980; Tinto 1975). These friendships or relationships can be between students and students, students and faculty, or students and administrators or staff. What appears to be of primary importance is that students need individuals on the campus whom they can talk to and feel comfortable with. Finding one or more persons who fill this need can increase each student's sense of integration into the campus environment and can enhance persistence.

## Involvement with the Campus

Students can be involved with the college campus in many ways. Generally, there is a positive relationship between retention and high levels of involvement. Lenning, Sauer, and Beal (1980a) state that extracurricular activities and recreation can have a positive effect on student retention as long as they are not overdone. The concept of social integration is a key element in the works of Spady (1970, 1972), Tinto (1975), Terenzini and Pascarella (1977, 1978, 1980) and Terenzini et al. (1981). Included within this concept of social integration is involvement in campus activities and events. Churchill and Iwai (1981) discovered that dropouts with low grade point averages were less likely to make use of student services and facilities. Astin (1975) found that participation in athletics and Greek organizations reduced the likelihood of dropping out. The evidence suggests that involvement and use of campus activities and facilities can have a positive effect upon student persistence.

## College Residence

Whether a student lives at home, in a university residence hall, in Greek housing, or away from home can influence student attrition. After examining the dropout rates at different kinds of institutions, Astin (1975) concludes that residential facilities are the most influential variable affecting retention rates. According to Astin, living at home produces the greatest likelihood of dropping out, while living in Greek housing results in even higher persistence rates than does living in campus residence halls. Moos (1979), however, looked at the effect of campus residency more carefully and found that women living in single-sex dormitories were more likely to persist than they were in coed dorms.

There is undoubtedly a relationship between college residence and the previously discussed variable of campus involvement. Students who live in college and university residence halls would be hard put to avoid greater involvement in campus activities. In addition, the conditions for establishing friendships with students, faculty, and staff are greater. Both variables contribute to the importance of living on campus as a retention factor.

## Financial Assistance

The type of financial assistance students receive to help them pursue higher education does have an impact on attrition rates. Although the results are somewhat mixed, it appears that receiving a scholarship or grant has a positive effect on persistence (Ramist 1981). The degree of effect is not clear; estimates range from 10 to 15 percentage points to 1 to 2 percent (p. 15).

Astin found that receiving loans had a negative impact on student retention, particularly among male students, where receiving loans resulted in a 6 percent increase in the chance of dropping out (p. 61). Conversely, he discovered that working on campus enhances persistence. Once again, this may be related to the fact that working on campus increases the student's involvement and enhances the likelihood of establishing some relationships at the institution.

Other financial aid factors that influence persistence include parental assistance, spouse support, and employment off campus. Generally, parental financial support reduces the dropout rate (Astin 1975). Freshmen who work full-time or part-time off campus are more likely to drop out (Astin 1975; Iffert 1958). Astin discovered that when spouse support exceeded 50 percent of the costs, the chances for persistence rose 28 percent for men and 15 percent for women (p. 54); however, if the amount is less than 50 percent, the effect of spouse support was to reduce the chances of graduation.

Thus, the impact of financial aid is varied and complex. The complexity highlights the need for each campus to have varied and differential aid policies targeted to meet the needs of a diverse student population.

The causes of attrition involve the characteristics of both student and institution, the match between the two sets of characteristics, and the way they interact with each other. As college administrators have learned more about the characteristics of nonpersisters and some of the causes of attrition, they have begun to develop programs designed to reduce the number of students who drop out.

## THE CURRENT STATUS OF RETENTION PROGRAMS

During the past 10 years the number of programs developed to reduce student attrition has increased rapidly. There are excellent overviews of retention programs, including *What Works in Student Retention?* by Beal and Noel; *Student Retention Strategies* by Lenning, Sauer, and Beal; and *College Student Attrition and Retention* by Ramist. One of the major problems with retention programs, however, is that frequently they have not been carefully evaluated to establish their effectiveness. All too often, colleges and universities have developed programs to reduce attrition and then simply implemented them. Such programs arise out of a perceived need, a general review of the literature on student retention, and the implementation of a tactic without any plans for monitoring and evaluating the strategy. As a result, one of the weaknesses of this section is the lack of evidence that the programs do indeed work.

The next part of this review provides an overview of those retention programs that appear to be most successful and also sets the stage for the chapter's final section, which examines new research trends and program implications for reducing student attrition.

## Admissions

Many retention programs begin with recruitment and admissions. As Chapter 5 demonstrated, matching the student with the institution, finding the right "fit," is an important element of the college-choice process and student persistence patterns. As Ott (in Noel 1978) asserts, one of the most important elements in a successful retention effort is the recruitment of graduates, as opposed to the simple recruitment of students. If enrollment managers make sure that their literature accurately portrays the college or university, if the admissions staff are trained to be counselors, and if institutional leadership is committed to attracting students who will match the goals of the college—attrition should be lessened. It is important to note, however, that although almost every comprehensive discussion of retention programs discusses the linkage between retention and "recruiting graduates," no research firmly documents the connection. This typifies some of the questions that require applied research for enrollment managers

## Orientation

In the national survey of retention programs conducted by Beal and Noel (1980), orientation was ranked the third most important retention activity. Orientation programs allow students to become acclimated to the campus and its environment. Such programs can help to encourage peer and faculty interactions, inform students about counseling and career guidance services, provide descriptions of financial aid assistance, and integrate students into the extracurricular life of the institution. All these factors, of course, have been found to be related to student persistence. Nevertheless, similar to the linkage of recruitment activities to retention, further research is needed to validate the relationship between effective orientation programs and reductions in student attrition.

## Advising and Freshman Seminar Programs

Student-faculty interaction is proving to be one of the most important variables in student attrition studies (Lenning, Sauer, and Beal 1980a,b; Terenzini and Pascarella 1977, 1980; Pascarella and Terenzini 1980a; Ramist 1981). As a result, many colleges and universities are creating structures that bring students and faculty together. For example, academic advising is a natural setting for student and faculty interaction. Faculty who are genuinely interested in student growth and development appear to influence persistence positively (Terenzini et al. 1981). Advising provides an excellent opportunity for faculty members to demonstrate their interest.

In addition to these programs, institutions are also developing special freshman courses and seminars. The work of Terenzini and Pascarella is especially supportive of this approach. Their research suggests that two kinds of faculty interaction are strongly correlated with continuance to graduation. Student-faculty interaction outside the class, which centers around course-related material and intellectual discussions, has a consistently positive relationship to persistence. Because many efforts of retention programs focus on the freshman year, numerous institutions have attempted to create situations where student-faculty interchange about course materials and intellectual matters would be more likely to occur. As a result, courses ranging from prolonged orientation to freshman seminars have been implemented. The common elements in these courses usually include a small student-faculty ratio, a discussion-oriented format, and faculty members recruited for their ability to relate to students.

## Counseling and Career Planning

These two functions are typically housed in the student services division of a college or university and are often located in close proximity. Both functions can be a part of a campus retention program.

Counseling offices can assist students with adjustment problems, issues of relationship and involvement, decision making, and problems of self-concept and motivation. Lenning, Sauer, and Beal (1980a,b) document several counseling programs that have reduced attrition, and they point out that counseling services can serve as the foundation for many retention activities.

Career-planning offices can also assist students in resolving some of their problems that concern career goals. Students often enter college without well-defined academic and/or career goals. The failure to develop such goals can lead to dropping out. Ramist (1981) noted that over 70 percent of the students with less than a C grade point average and more than 30 percent of the nonacademic dropouts cited a lack of certainty about future goals as the reason they were leaving school (p. 20). It appears that career-planning centers can play an important role in assisting these undecided students.

## Learning Assistance Centers

As colleges have increasingly admitted both students of lesser ability and underprepared matriculants, the need for academic assistance has rapidly increased. Because academic success in college is related to persistence, many campuses have found it wise to develop centers to assist these students. Learning assistance centers often provide services such as reading enhancement, tutoring, study skills and test-taking sessions, as well as monitoring the academic progress of students identified as academically at high risk.

## Residence Life and Extracurricular Activities

As stated previously under College Residence, Astin (1975) asserts that living in a residence hall is the most influential environmental factor affecting persistence. He also found that involvement in campus activities improved retention. For both variables the key is student-to-student interaction, which is greatly enhanced by living in residence halls and being involved in campus events. Terenzini and Pascarella (1977, 1980) and Bean (1983) also found that the degree of social integration experienced by each student positively affected persistence. Thus, it seems that institutions of higher education are wise to maintain strong extracurricular programs and to emphasize the benefits of residential living (if they own residence halls). It may be beneficial for all campuses to attempt to create an institutional "press" that emphasizes peer involvement and interaction.

## Campus Employment

As a result of Astin's findings, colleges and universities are increasing their efforts to create jobs for students on their campuses. Some are using institutional funds to create more jobs (Hodgkinson 1982). Other colleges are watching their hiring practices more carefully to ensure that some students do not end up with two or three on-campus jobs while others are unable to find employment. Yet another model is Berea College in Berea, Kentucky, where all students must work on the campus to help perform necessary functions, as well as on income-producing activities.

## Exit Interviews

An important part of any retention effort is gathering data about persisting and nonpersisting students. Enrollment managers need to know why students leave. Exit interviews with dropouts can help to clarify their reasons for leaving and can provide information that can be used to initiate new academic and social programs as well as to make adjustments in existing ones.

An often overlooked aspect of exit interviews is the value of interviewing graduates as well as withdrawers. The graduates can inform a campus of its best and most satisfying features. They can also prevent an institution from changing a program disliked by some dropouts but greatly valued by the graduates. In addition, graduating-student interviews can be an excellent vehicle for providing positive feedback and reinforcement to those campus areas that are meeting or exceeding the needs of students.

## Early-Warning and Attrition-Alert Systems

Colleges and universities have initiated programs designed to identify in advance those students most likely to drop out. Early-warning systems permit administrators to recognize potential dropouts and devise intervention strategies before the students make the decision to drop out.

Attrition-alert systems can take many forms. One potential approach is to work with students who are on academic probation. Another is to assist students who have received two or more unsatisfactory grade notices at the midpoint of the grading period. Creating an informal network of faculty, administrators, staff, and students who are asked to refer the names of students who appear to be isolated or give other signs of needing help can also serve as an attrition-alert system. Perhaps the most objective systems are those built around a questionnaire with the ability to reliably predict nonpersisters. The most promising efforts in this area have been made by Terenzini and Pascarella. Although several other instruments have been developed for individual campuses, Terenzini and Pascarella have used their model on more than one campus and have replicated their research several times. They have been able to successfully identify persisters and withdrawers in advance with accuracy ranging from 60 to 80 percent (Terenzini and Pascarella 1977, 1980; Terenzini et al. 1981). This questionnaire holds great promise but should be tested at more campuses of different size and control. The ability to identify potential dropouts accurately in advance should greatly improve the effectiveness of retention efforts.

Retention programs have become a fixture on many campuses. Some programmatic thrusts have been proved to be effective; others remain to be validated. Many programs are based on research, but have not actually been evaluated at the institutional level. The necessity for this evaluation becomes more evident in the next section.

## A THEORETICAL PERSPECTIVE

Thus far, this discussion has synthesized many studies, most of which have lacked a theoretical perspective and have tended to be applied in nature. While this does not negate the value of such efforts, a theoretical base can provide the foundation for a more comprehensive and individualized approach to the issue of student retention. Several theories have been advanced to explain the process of student attrition (Bean 1983; Cope and Hannah 1975; Rootman 1972; Spady 1970; Tinto 1975). At the moment the two theories that appear to hold the most promise are Tinto's Student Integration Model (1975) and Bean's Industrial Model of Student Attrition (1983). Bean has been in the process of developing his model since 1978, and Terenzini and Pascarella have been working with Tinto's model since 1976. Since both models help to set the stage for further work in retention, both are briefly explained.

## Student Integration Model

The Student Integration Model (see Figure 9) builds upon Spady's model of student attrition (1970). Tinto asserts that colleges are made up of two domains—the social and the academic. Academic integration reflects the direct relationship between higher education and future occupational attainment. Social integration refers to campus activities and college life. The greater the level of integration in these two domains, the less likely a student is to drop out of that institution. Both domains, however, are environmental. As a result, Tinto also includes the matriculants' background characteristics, which comprise socioeconomic status, high school experiences, community of residence, ability, educational plans and aspirations, and motivation. Tinto speculates that educational goal commitment may be the most important dimension if all other factors are equal.

The model permits the consideration of a number of variables. For instance, goal commitment can include individual responses to the labor market, such as those discussed in Chapter 2 of this work. Individual attributes allow for different levels of motivation. Perhaps most important, the model explains how different persons can perceive the same situation in different ways.

## Industrial Model of Student Attrition

Bean takes an industrial model of turnover in work organizations and applies it to colleges and universities (see Figure 10). The assumption is that students and employees may leave their respective organizations for similar reasons. The model contains 12 determinants and 2 intervening variables. The 12 determinants are the following:

1. Grades—the student's college grade point average
2. Practical value—the belief that one's education will lead to a career
3. Development—the desire for self-development
4. Routinization—repetitive work
5. Instrumental communication—being informed about issues on the campus

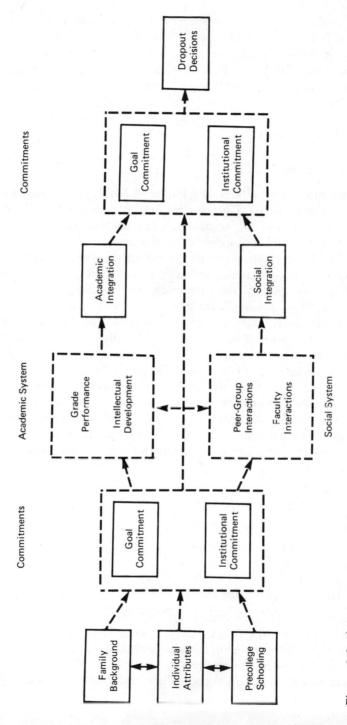

**Figure 9** Student integration model.

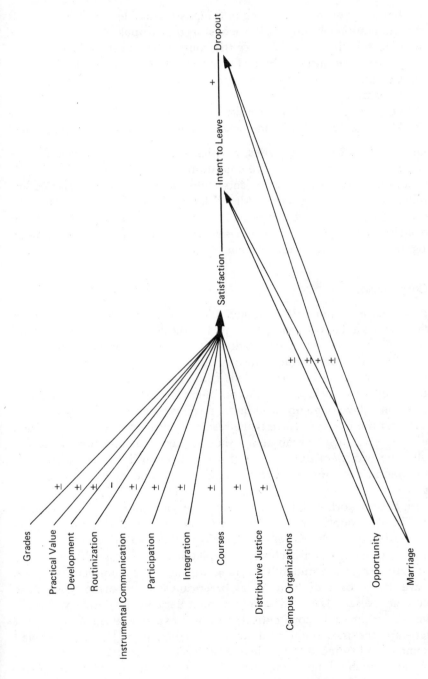

**Figure 10** Industrial model of student attrition.

6. Participation—participating in campus-related decisions
7. Integration—having close friends on the campus
8. Courses—being able to take the courses one wants to take
9. Distributive justice—being fairly treated on the campus
10. Campus organizations—the number of memberships in campus organizations
11. Opportunity—the opportunity to transfer
12. Marriage—the likelihood that a student will marry before graduation

Note that Bean considers grades, practical value, and development to be the extrinsic rewards of a college education.

In addition to these determinants, the two intervening variables are satisfaction and intent to leave. All 12 determinants influence satisfaction positively or negatively. Satisfaction, in turn, affects intent to leave. Bean also includes background variables similar to those in the Tinto model, recognizing that these factors influence persistence.

## A Comparison

The models have much in common. Background variables are a part of both. Although Tinto's concept of integration differs from that of Bean's model (Tinto's concept of integration is the more comprehensive of the two), if Bean's factors of grades, instrumental communication, participation, and campus organizations are included, the two theories are very similar. Both theories also include the concepts of grades, intellectual development, and personal development. In addition, there is a similarity between Bean's notion that the intent to leave is the result of all the preceding factors and Tinto's assertion that commitment is the product of the preceding variables. Finally, the two theories recognize that the dropout decision is a complex phenomenon resulting from the interaction of student and institutional factors.

Both Bean's work with his model and Terenzini and Pascarella's research with Tinto's model come to the conclusion that goal commitment and intent to leave are the strongest predictors. The two theories differ considerably, though, when it comes to explaining the factors that exert the most influence on the student's reaching this stage of commitment or intent to leave. Bean concludes that grades, practical value, opportunity, marriage (note that the sample included only women because the author was replicating an earlier study done entirely with nurses), and satisfaction—in that order—are the most influential variables (1983, p. 141). Pascarella and Chapman (1983) find that the degree of academic integration is the most important variable influencing persistence at commuter institutions. Conversely, at residential campuses social integration appears to be more strongly related to continuance (Terenzini and Pascarella 1984).

At this point there is no simple explanation for the differences between the results of the studies conducted by Bean and those by Pascarella and Terenzini. Because the instrument devised by Pascarella and Terenzini has been used more frequently, their work has been more systematic. As they have worked with Tinto's model and their own instrument, however, they have increasingly become more cautious in their interpretations of the results. Recent writings of Pascarella, Terenzini, and others point out the complexity of attrition. Furthermore, they suggest that the model may need revisions or that the concepts of academic and social integration have not been adequately operationalized.

## IMPROVING RETENTION RESEARCH AND EVALUATION

Student attrition has been a concern on many campuses for several years, and therefore a number of instruments and services have evolved to assist colleges and universities. Both the American College Testing Program and the College Board, in conjunction with the National Center for Higher Education Management Systems (NCHEMS), market instruments designed to be given to withdrawing students. The purpose of these instruments is to help institutions identify the factors that have preceded the student's decision to withdraw. The College Board/NCHEMS survey, the Former Student Questionnaire, is part of the Student Outcomes Information Service. The ACT instrument, the Withdrawing Student Questionnaire, is part of the Evaluation Survey Service. Both the College Board and ACT can also provide scoring and data analysis services.

In addition to survey instruments, the College Board, as part of its Admissions Testing Program–Summary Reporting Service (ATP-SRS), can provide participating institutions with information on the characteristics of persisting and withdrawing students as they move through their collegiate experience. The Council of Independent Colleges also has a retention analysis service available for small campuses that are just beginning to examine their attrition rates. All of these various services can be of use to enrollment managers who are attempting to develop a campus-based retention program.

While many colleges have started to collect information on persisting and withdrawing students, this has often been the extent of their efforts in this area. Few institutions of higher learning have carefully evaluated the efficacy of their retention programs. Typically, the administrators charged with monitoring student persistence do not have the time or perhaps the ability to analyze these programs carefully. Generally, evaluations of retention activities have lacked the necessary staff, skills, or interest to assess the effectiveness of such programs accurately. Boyd et al. (1982) suggest a "stepwise" plan for the evaluation of retention programs:

1. Generate a pool of information concerning attrition and retention from a review of relevant literature, as well as discussions and brainstorming sessions with knowledgeable campus members. These activities are aimed at achieving the following objectives:

   a. Identifying an array of specific interventions that seem potentially useful in reducing attrition rates among given subgroups of students.

   b. Developing categories that depict arrays of different subgroups of students with whom certain interventions have been used or seem to warrant usage.

2. Devise a series of research studies employing different interventions with distinct subgroups of small-sample clusters held constant, vary the different interventions, and record effects.

3. Enlist the cooperation of campus offices, individuals, or programs whose cooperation would be crucial to the implementation of these studies.

4. Implement the studies of various interventions on a small-sample basis with control groups. Conduct several small-sample studies concurrently.

5. Closely evaluate outcomes over at least a two-to-six-year period in terms of behavioral criteria of retention-attrition.

6. ... The above assessments should allow for optimal combining and sequencing of multiple interventions for various subgroups (pp. 392–93).

A stepwise plan such as this can allow an institution to analyze retention activities more carefully and to implement effective programs.

## IMPROVING STUDENT RETENTION: INDIVIDUALIZATION AND TARGETING

Perhaps the most important inferences to be gleaned from these recent efforts come from some of the conclusions of Terenzini and Pascarella (1980, pp. 280–281). They conclude:

1. Reliable predictions of attrition on the basis of precollege traits cannot be made.

2. What happens to students after they arrive on campus and the manner in which those experiences interact with prematriculation traits are the most important elements of the student attrition process.

As the result of the attention given to the characteristics of entering matriculants and the qualities of the individual campuses, a sense of futility often settles in. This sense of futility might best be described by the following statement: "Given the kinds of students we attract and the type of institution we are, our attrition rate may well be a fact of life we must learn to accept."

The work of Pascarella and Terenzini, however, suggests that this may not be the case. Their finding that neither the background characteristics of the matriculants nor the qualities of the college or university alone enable reliable predictions of persistence is important. The implications of these results are that institutions of all types can do more to improve student persistence. Pascarella and Terenzini's work is important from another perspective, too. Institutions of higher education are in the business of teaching and advancing knowledge. The knowledge that student-faculty interaction can play an important role in retaining students is both reassuring and important.

The awareness that student persistence can be determined by the inter-action of student and environment brings us back full circle to the discussion in Chapter 5 of student-institution fit. This research also suggests that each institution must more carefully examine how students are interacting with the environment in order to discover the likely targets of retention-intervention programs. This identification of likely target groups of non-persisters is a process similar in many ways to the steps required of enrollment managers to identify potential matriculants.

In the future, colleges and universities, if they are to continue to improve their retention efforts, will have to develop more sophisticated tools to identify potential dropouts and their needs. It may well be that an instrument like the one developed by Pascarella and Terenzini will have to be modified and adapted to be useful for different campuses with different students and environments. Colleges and universities may find that their persisters and dropouts can be segmented into different groups, just as their potential markets are segmented.

Lewis, Leach, and Lutz (1983) state that the basis for marketing and student retention programs have a great deal in common. The purpose of both activities, they suggest, is to improve the congruity of fit between the student and the campus. On large campuses it will probably make more sense to talk about the subenvironments of certain disciplines, schools, or residence groupings. On smaller campuses the segmented groups would undoubtedly be less diverse, but subgroups can still exist. In much the same way that institutions of higher learning develop targeted recruitment strategies to maintain or improve enrollments, targeted retention strategies may be necessary to improve persistence rates.

Successful enrollment management necessitates an understanding of why students come to a campus and why they stay. Effective nonprofit marketing research can be utilized on both campus populations and potential campus populations. Reaching the market segments of potential dropouts requires no less research and evaluation than the efforts expended to attract students.

## SUGGESTIONS FOR FURTHER READING

*Preventing Students from Dropping Out,* by A. W. Astin.

"The Application of a Model of Turnover in Work Organizations to the Student Attrition Process," by John P. Bean.

*Student Retention Strategies,* by Oscar T. Lenning, Kenneth Sauer, and Phillip E. Beal.

"Predicting Freshman Persistence and Voluntary Dropout Decisions from a Theoretical Model," by Ernest T. Pascarella and Patrick T. Terenzini.

*College Student Attrition and Retention,* by Leonard Ramist.

"Dropout from Higher Education: A Theoretical Synthesis of Recent Research," by J. Vincent Tinto.

# PART THREE

This last part examines the impact and outcomes of higher learning in the United States. Students and parents alike have increasingly come to view the college enrollment decision as an investment decision. As consumers of higher education, they seek the institution that will offer them the best return on the investment of their time, labor, and capital. There is an impressive volume of evidence that going to college does make a difference in the lives of those who attend, in addition to enriching American society.

Despite this established research base, there is little evidence that college and university administrators make use of these findings in their decisions and day-to-day activities. For enrollment managers, the task is to develop more knowledgeable and sophisticated ways to communicate with these "new" consumers of higher education. Chapters 7 and 8 acquaint enrollment managers with literature describing the impact and outcomes of college attendance. This provides a context for decisions and helps to set the institutional research agenda on individual campuses.

## Chapter 7

# The Impact of College on Students

### THE SIGNIFICANCE OF IMPACT STUDIES

The effect of college on students is responsible for an important body of knowledge that enrollment managers should be familiar with for several reasons. This knowledge enables colleges and universities to articulate more clearly the benefits of a college degree. If a college knows the specific impact it has on its students, the marketing efforts of the enrollment management office should be more effective. Some of the findings derived from impact studies can also be used to improve institutional retention efforts.

The use of ethical marketing practices in higher education calls on the directors of enrollment management efforts to market the campus as it is actually experienced by current students. Chapter 5 has discussed student-institution fit and the relationship between fit and persistence. Familiarity with the effects of college on students, if used in marketing materials and strategies, can help to assure that the college is accurately portrayed. Accurate representations should help to improve the college-choice process for students and for colleges and universities.

Finally, understanding the effects of college on students can provide a perspective for enrollment managers and other administrative decision makers. Such knowledge can be used in campus planning to inform decisions in many different areas of the institution. Perhaps most important, such research promotes institutional self-understanding, which is worthwhile in and of itself. Litten, Sullivan, and Brodigan (1983) state this well in their recent book, *Applying Market Research in College Admissions:* "Furthermore, colleges promote the ideal that self-understanding is good in itself, that basic insights into the nature of the world are of value even though their particular utility may not be foreseeable. This is especially true in a rapidly changing world, where changes in the financial or social infrastructure or the marketing initiatives of competitors can substantially and suddenly alter the order of things" (p. 34).

This chapter begins by examining the strengths and weaknesses—the limitations—of impact studies. This is important to ensure that enrollment managers do not overstate the benefits or liabilities of a college education. The reason students change while in college is briefly explained. This can be useful to enrollment managers who wish to bring about changes in the socialization process on their campuses, or who wish to manage the campus environment more effectively.

After this review of student impact models, the pattern that characterizes student experiences from prematriculation to graduation is examined, followed by a discussion of the cognitive and noncognitive effects of college. The chapter then analyzes how different types of institutional factors affect different types of students. Finally, instruments and methodologies for measuring college impact are explored. The intent is to offer guidelines for enrollment managers who wish to conduct impact studies on their campuses.

## THE LIMITATIONS OF IMPACT RESEARCH

Enrollment managers should have a sense of the limitations in the conclusions derived from the study of college effects on students. Some strengths and weaknesses are the result of the period during which the studies were conducted. Other limitations reflect the current boundaries of research methodologies and the ways the results are traditionally reported.

Most early research on college students was on samples of white males, ages 18 to 21, because until recently women, minorities, and older nontraditional students did not attend colleges and universities in large numbers. Only current studies are likely to include these new arrivals to higher education. There is also a paucity of research on the effects of two-year colleges. Most research has been conducted on four-year college campuses. Another problem with much of the research is that it was conducted during the 1960s and mid-1970s, a time of turmoil and change in society as well as on most campuses. With the perspective of time it is apparent that this period was not the norm for United States higher education but was rather an aberration. Many studies that deal with political and social attitudes during this period may no longer be accurate.

In methodological issues, there is the ongoing debate concerning the virtues of cross-sectional research as opposed to longitudinal studies. Given the time and costs involved, most research uses a cross-sectional approach. In addition, social scientists must ask whether most changes are the result of student maturation or are produced by the college experience. While it seems true that the characteristics, attitudes, and abilities of matriculants influence the changes they experience in college, it appears equally true that the college experience itself has an effect on student lives. Another problem with most impact findings is pointed out by Bowen (1977, pp. 28–29). He notes that most research looks at the mean or average change scores for an entire sample of college students. If this procedure is followed, the individual change scores of the subjects are lost. Thus, both a student who demonstrates a large positive change and one who shows a small negative change in achievement motivation are lost in a mean score that reveals a slight increase in achievement motivation for the entire sample.

A final caution for enrollment managers is that this chapter summarizes the findings of research conducted at many kinds of institutions. The results reported are generally true, but may or may not describe a specific institution. One purpose of the chapters on impact and outcomes is to make the existing literature more readily available to enrollment managers. Another purpose, however, is to demonstrate the need for institutional research on individual campuses so that enrollment planners can have access to data that will enable them to do their jobs more effectively.

Despite the reservations described in the preceding paragraphs, the research on student impact is important and worthwhile. Regardless of the varied methodological approaches and the differences in the samples gathered and the instruments used, there is a great deal of consistency among the findings of many topics examined. There appears to be ample evidence that higher education does indeed make a difference.

The difference is the result of the interaction of individual student and campus characteristics. As indicated in Figure 11, these factors interact to produce the impact and outcomes of higher education that are discussed in the remainder of this chapter and in Chapter 8. The model in Figure 11 provides a conceptual frame of reference for enrollment managers as they attempt to understand and facilitate student development.

## A FOUR-YEAR PROFILE

### The Freshman Year

Certain characteristics and experiences appear to typify the passage through collegiate life. As discussed in Chapter 3, before matriculation most freshmen do not have a clear idea of what college will be like. Most students are not prepared for the demands of college. At entrance they expect to do well academically and anticipate that their intellectual experiences will be a major source of satisfaction for them (Feldman and Newcomb 1969).

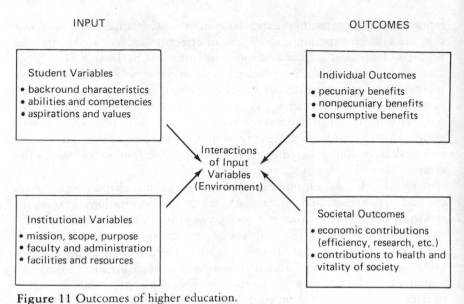

**Figure 11** Outcomes of higher education.

In contrast, Davis and Cloakey (in Feldman and Newcomb 1969, p. 83), in a study of 13,000 students at 23 different institutions, note that only 47 percent of the sample actually found their intellectual experiences to be their major source of satisfaction. Many entering freshmen find they have to lower their expectations.

For the typical new matriculant, there will be a wide variety of new experiences and many decisions to be made. Harnqvist (1978) points out that the decision to pursue higher eduction and the subsequent decisions regarding course selection, new friends, and so forth, are perhaps the first decisions students make on their own. Feldman and Newcomb make the following observations: Entering freshmen are usually anxious about academic success and often experience culture shock after coming into contact with the campus; initially these new students typically spread a wide net, attempting to bring in as many friends as possible, for sheer proximity can be an important determinant in the establishment of early friendships. Freshmen also enter expecting to have significant relationships and frequent contact with faculty. In reality, they interact with faculty less than do their returning classmates (Astin 1977; Feldman and Newcomb 1969).

## The Sophomore and Junior Years

After the first year in college, students begin to adapt to the campus. Again, drawing from Feldman and Newcomb, nonfreshmen can be described as more relaxed about their studies. They become increasingly selective about their friends; shared interests and values become more important. Peer solidarity begins to build and becomes most important during the junior year.

The sophomore year, in particular, is an interesting year; research finding here have implications for enrollment managers. When sophomores return to campus, the enthusiasm and excitement of the first year has dissipated. According to Kenniston and Helmreich (in Feldman and Newcomb 1969, p. 92), cynicism and dissatisfaction characterize the sophomore year. These students often feel neglected by the institution and perceive themselves to be treated less like adults than they were as freshmen. Feldman and Newcomb conclude that these findings are consistent with a number of other studies, all of which point to the existence of a "sophomore slump." The implications are that some sophomores may drop out during this "slump" because their dissatisfaction leads them to believe that they are at the wrong institution. These sophomores, however, might be dissatisfied no matter what college or university they were attending. Enrollment managers need to develop retention programs with this in mind, perhaps even educating sophomore students about the nature of this potential slump.

## The Senior Year

During the senior year students begin to pull away from the institution. The differences between men and women decline during the entire four years and reach their lowest point in the senior year (Astin 1977; Kent and Astin 1983). The number of close friendships diminishes and interests tend to become more solitary and personal (Bowen 1977; Feldman and Newcomb 1969). In findings that are similar to the research showing overestimations of ability at entrance, Baird (1973) notes that a large percentage of graduating seniors rate themselves in the top 10 percent in the areas of skills relating to others, sympathy for others in trouble, perseverance, and reliability (p. 36). Seniors are more likely to engage in cultural activities, to read unassigned books, and to be more autonomous and independent (Astin 1977; Baird 1973; Bowen 1977; Feldman and Newcomb 1969; Winter et al. 1981).

The stages a student moves through while attending college do appear to follow a pattern. Understanding this pattern can be useful to enrollment managers. It can provide insights into the campus environment that can assist college administrators who wish to change or more effectively manage the environment. Knowledge of the cycle can be of value to counseling personnel, student activities staff, as well as those concerned about retention. All these areas are part of a comprehensive enrollment management plan.

## THE EFFECTS OF COLLEGE ON NONCOGNITIVE GROWTH

Astin (1977) states there are two types of growth that take place while the student is in college. One is cognitive and includes both the knowledge base the student develops and the increase in intellectual capacity (the ease with which a student learns new ideas and critical thinking). The second is noncognitive and refers to changes that occur in such areas as student values and attitudes, the competencies students develop in their abilities to interact with others, the interests they develop, and the way they choose to spend their leisure time. In this section the noncognitive effects of college attendance are reviewed. A discussion of the cognitive effects follows.

### Beliefs and Attitudes

Beliefs and attitudes constitute an area where research has demonstrated that college attendance has a significant and consistent effect. This research, conducted over a number of years and employing a wide variety of methodologies, has shown that college students appear to emerge from their experience more open and tolerant, less dogmatic and authoritarian, and less ethnocentric (Astin 1977; Bowen 1977; Feldman and Newcomb 1969; Trent and Medsker 1968). It appears, too, that the exposure to new ideas and to a more diverse group of peers brings about changes in beliefs and attitudes.

The bulk of the studies conducted in the 1960s through the mid-1970s also suggested that college students were more altruistic and more likely to be involved in political issues and community action groups (Bowen 1977; Feldman and Newcomb 1969; Trent and Medsker 1968). Solmon and Oschner (1978), however, assert that this is no longer the case. There has been an increased concern for financial security among all students and a corresponding decreased interest in politics—in becoming a political candidate or becoming involved in community action projects (pp. 8–9). Solmon and Oschner further believe that there has been an increase in narcissism among students. Many of these changes are also reflected in the political changes discussed later.

### Religious Beliefs

Another consistently reported impact of college is on the religious values and activities of students. Most research reveals a decline in religious orthodoxy and in the acceptance of religious dogma among college students (Bowen 1977; Feldman and Newcomb 1969; Ramist 1981; Trent and Medsker 1968). Astin (1977) also describes a decline in church attendance, prayer, and other outward signs of religiosity. These results are affected by the characteristics of students upon entrance and are influenced by the kind of institution attended. Nevertheless, the overall impact of college on religiosity is to diminish the role it plays in the lives of college students.

## Maturity, Self-Confidence, and Self-Esteem

Virtually all studies show that seniors leave college with a greater sense of self-confidence and self-esteem than they had when they entered (Kent and Astin 1983; Astin 1977; Bowen 1977; Feldman and Newcomb 1969; Winter et al. 1981). Winter et al. found that participation in athletics and voluntary service involvement increased students' sense of independence and self-definition as well as their range of self-rated abilities. Attending selective colleges also seems to enhance students' self-esteem (Astin 1977). Winter et al., in their study of a liberal arts education, speculate that institutions that help to give students a sense of being special facilitate the development of independence, self-esteem, and self-confidence.

Similarly, college seniors demonstrate higher levels of maturity than do entering freshmen or non–college-going peers (Bowen 1977; Feldman and Newcomb 1969; Trent and Medsker 1968; Winter et al. 1981). Winter et al. note that exposure to new ideas and increased levels of participation in cultural and extracurricular activities appear to be related to higher levels of maturity. From this evidence it seems clear that attending a college or university does lead to greater levels of maturity as well as enhanced levels of self-confidence and autonomy.

## Political Values

Until recently almost all research indicated that college seniors were more politically liberal than entering freshmen or their non–college-going peers (Astin 1977; Boldt and Stroud 1934; Bowen 1977; Feldman and Newcomb 1969; Schuster and Coil 1982; Ramist 1981; Trent and Medsker 1968; Wilson and Gaff 1975). Astin writes that increases in liberalism are associated with having Jewish parents, being a black male, being Roman Catholic or having no religious preference, having high academic ability, being altruistic, having a high artistic interest, being hedonistic, and enjoying drinking. Movements toward greater conservatism are associated with being female, being older than the average student, having higher scores on interest in religion, and having strong business interests (p. 37).

Much of the research cited, however, was gathered from the 1960s to the mid-1970s. The zeitgeist, or spirit of the times, has clearly changed. Astin is aware of this and cautions that specific attitudinal changes are more likely to be the result of societal forces than of individual institutions. The works of Levine (1980) and Solmon and Oschner (1978) suggest that the political values of more recent college students have clearly changed. Levine speaks wistfully about the political idealism of the 1960s. Solmon and Oschner, in their sample of college seniors, find them more likely to be middle-of-the-road politically. The authors suggest that the large switch from the social sciences and humanities to business and the hard sciences accounts for much of this shift, since these disciplines are typically more conservative (p. 10). Such conclusions are supported by the work of Endo and Harpel (1980), who note that students in professional and liberal arts programs differed on a number of dimensions. Solmon and Oschner conclude that the shift from conservative to liberal documented by Feldman and Newcomb and Bowen no longer appears to be borne out.

## Leadership

For some students, at least, attending a college or university appears to affect their ability and interest in taking on leadership positions. Winter et al. (1981) found, once again, that this sense of being special seemed to encourage the development of greater leadership motivation (p. 146). Being involved in athletics also facilitated leadership. At least at one institution the authors found that students who expressed the greatest initial degree of frustration also experienced the greatest amount of growth in several areas, including leadership motivation (p. 143). Kent and Astin (1983) note a positive relationship between leadership experiences and the students' perceptions of their academic ability, their leadership ability, and their public speaking ability (p. 315). Endo and Harpel (1980) document that business schools place more emphasis on participation in extracurricular activities and the acquisition of leadership skills when compared with liberal arts programs. The findings suggest that college can have an impact on the development of leadership skills among students.

## Cultural and Aesthetic Values

College appears to have an effect on the cultural and aesthetic values of students. Feldman and Newcomb (1969) note that college seniors are more likely to attend lectures and cultural events (p. 96). They also state that college seems to raise the aesthetic value scores of students on the Allport-Vernon-Lindzey Study of Value (p. 8). Endo and Harpel (1980) reveal that liberal arts students are more interested in creativity. College students are more likely to read unassigned books and cultural magazines and to attend concerts, public lectures, and art exhibits (Trent and Medsker 1968, pp. 143–144). These differences between college attenders and nonattenders are generally supported in both impact and outcome studies. Bowen (1977) concludes that college "does, on the average, raise the perception or appreciation of the fine arts and literature" (p. 83). In cultural and intellectual pursuits, however, he is more cautious, concluding that higher education does have some impact on the intellectual and cultural pursuits of students, but that the degree of significance of the change is hard to determine (p. 88).

## Career Orientation

College may have some effect on the career motivations of students, but the exact nature of these effects is difficult to determine. Feldman and Newcomb (1969) find little consistency among the results in this area. Some findings show that college seniors are more success-oriented than are entering freshmen. Other works suggest that seniors are less interested in success than are entering freshmen (pp. 17–18). Part of this problem stems from what is being measured. Freshmen are more likely to rate a job important as an external source of security. Seniors, on the other hand, are more oriented toward self-expression and view a job as an outlet for self-expression (pp. 17–18). Bowen (1977) concludes that college generally raises the aspirations of students and that college students tend to become increasingly concerned about the intrinsic factors of the job (p. 109). More recently Kent and Astin (1983) write that both men and women seem to become more interested in power and status as they move from their freshman to their senior year. More research is needed in this area to determine if a more difficult job market has changed the impact of college on interest in self-expression and the intrinsic values in a career.

## THE COGNITIVE OUTCOMES

Following this overview of the noncognitive effects of higher education, it is important to examine the cognitive benefits. Higher education institutions create and pass on knowledge and culture. Since this is their primary purpose, evidence should be available to demonstrate that students' capacities in this area are enhanced by attendance. Surprisingly, however, more research has been conducted on noncognitive than on cognitive development. What follows is an overview of the available research.

## Critical Thinking and Rationality

One of the often stated goals of higher education is an increase in the ability to analyze critically and to think rationally. Generally, findings in this area are inconclusive. Wilson and Gaff (1975) state that fewer than half of the seniors showed gains in their intellectual disposition on the Omnibus Personality Inventory (OPI). These results are consistent with those cited in Feldman and Newcomb (1969); their research revealed mixed findings on this scale of the OPI. Bowen (1977), however, urges caution in interpreting these results (p. 72). He notes that most of the institutions reporting no change or losses in intellectual disposition are very selective. He suggests that students at such colleges and universities score so high at entrance that there is little room for improvement (the "ceiling effect"). Keeley et al. (1982) write that seniors do evidence improvements in critical thinking. Their research demonstrates that seniors perform better at critically analyzing material when their directions are relatively open (which the authors consider to be the more demanding task). Interestingly, they perform at a lower level when the directions are more detailed and structured (p. 151).

In their work Winter et al. (1981) discovered that students at liberal arts colleges show improvement on the Test of Thematic Analysis; on the other hand, students at community colleges showed no improvement (pp. 62–63). The authors tried to measure the students' gain in learning new material, but found no differences between freshmen and seniors. They did, nevertheless, find that seniors demonstrated large gains in their ability to analyze arguments. At some institutions the gains were sixfold (p. 66).

Clearly, such results do not present a persuasive case for higher education and its impact on critical thinking and rationality. There appear to be some areas where attending college does make a difference, but the skills and competencies that students bring at entrance may be equally important in this area.

## Intellectual Awareness and General Knowledge

In United States colleges and universities, one of the goals of higher education has been to provide a broad general base of knowledge, to create an intellectual awareness of the milieu in which individuals and society function. In this regard institutions of higher learning seem to be meeting their expectations with success. After reviewing major studies on learning outcomes conducted over the past 50 years, Pace (1979) provides ample evidence that college students do make significant gains in the area of general knowledge. Bowen (1977) asserts that students demonstrate important improvements in their verbal and quantitative skills. Both Bowen (p. 68) and Pace (p. 78) document a tendency for students who take only one or two mathematics or science courses in college to show a decline in tests measuring mathematical or science skills.

Most research concludes that higher education positively affects intellectual awareness. Feldman and Newcomb (1969) found that seniors are more likely to engage in self-directed intellectual activity (p. 29). Evidence already presented in the areas of cultural awareness and critical thinking generally supports Bowen's conclusion that "on the average, higher education raises the level of . . . intellectual disposition and the cognitive powers of its students" (p. 98).

## Specialized Knowledge

Here again the findings are convincing that college seniors, as expected, learn a great deal about the areas in which they choose to specialize. Pace (1979) reviews several large research projects that show that seniors demonstrate the greatest growth in their areas of emphasis. In at least one study, students who had taken nine or more courses in a certain area consistently knew more about that subject than did those who had taken fewer than nine courses (p. 32). It is important to acknowledge that students, of necessity, will let some areas of intellectual growth hold steady or decline as they begin to specialize. Students cannot keep abreast of all knowledge areas.

In total, the results of the limited research conducted on the impact of college on cognitive development indicate that colleges and universities are generally quite successful. Students do develop a general knowledge base from which to draw, they do develop improved verbal skills, and they do demonstrate significant gains in their areas of specialization.

## THE DIFFERENTIAL IMPACTS OF COLLEGES AND UNIVERSITIES

To this point, this literature review has given an overview of the effects of college on students. There is ample evidence to demonstrate that the impacts of college can vary according to such variables as the type of institution attended, the amount of interaction students have with faculty, or whether the campus is primarily a residential or a commuter institution. One of the glaring absences in this section is any mention of the different impacts of two- and four-year colleges. Except for a few findings in Astin's book *Four Critical Years* (1977), there is simply not enough research yet available to make those kinds of comparisons. For enrollment managers to fully appreciate college impact and for them to be able to make the best use of impact studies, they should be aware of these different effects.

## The Effects of Faculty Interaction

The importance of student-faculty interaction has already been described in Chapter 6 on retention. The work of Pascarella and Terenzini, in particular, suggests that faculty can play an important role in the lives of students. Feldman and Newcomb (1973) state that most students want to have a significant relationship with faculty members. Astin (1977) notes that the desire on the part of students for interaction with the faculty increases each year they are in college. Generally, there is a relationship between the amount of student-faculty interaction and the level of student satisfaction with the college experience (Endo and Harpel 1981; Wilson and Gaff 1975; Pascarella and Terenzini 1980). As the amount of interaction increases, so does the level of satisfaction. Wilson and Gaff report a positive association between the amount, duration, and closeness of interaction, as well as the degree of assistance from faculty, and the career decisions of students (p. 133). Thistlewaite and Wheeler (1966) write that higher degrees of student-faculty interaction increased the possibility that the student would plan to go to graduate school. Feldman and Newcomb also conclude that faculty contact has a positive effect on the aspirations and career plans of college students. Wilson and Gaff describe a positive relationship between the amount of student-faculty interaction and the degree of intellectuality on the part of students.

In addition, Endo and Harpel (1981) come to the conclusion that the kind of faculty interaction makes a difference. Friendly interaction has more overall effect on students than does formal interaction (p. 15). Friendly interaction increases the student's level of satisfaction with the educational experience and exerts influence on the social and personal outcomes of higher education. The authors, however, find no relationship between friendly or formal interaction and academic achievement. It is also worth noting that Endo and Harpel describe faculty in professional schools as less likely to engage in friendly interaction than are faculty members in liberal arts programs.

Research on student-faculty interaction points to the important role the faculty can play in student satisfaction with the college experience and in student aspirations and career plans. The positive effect on persistence was previously documented. Feldman and Newcomb write:

> The teacher can be a critic, a rigorous and impartial judge of mental efforts; he can define standards of aspirations and of achievement. He can encourage a student's serious aspirations and strengthen his confidence in his own talent. . . .

The teacher may be a catalyst . . . and help him develop more fully his own proclivities and potentialities (p. 251).

## Student Peer Cultures

A student's peer culture can also have a strong impact on the student's development. Feldman and Newcomb (1969) suggest that peer orientations and values exert a strong influence on students. Peer cultures can support the goals and mission of an institution, thus enhancing the institution's efforts, or they can fail to support the goals, thus subverting and altering such efforts. Feldman and Newcomb describe the relationship between individual students and their peer groups as "reciprocal" and mutually reinforcing (p. 246). In terms of an institutional "press," they suggest that colleges are most successful in their intellectual goals when the enrolled students are committed to these goals (p. 261).

Clark and Trow (1966) hypothesize that student subcultures help to shape the beliefs and attitudes of the students belonging to these groups. They further speculate that on small campuses, one or two of these subcultures will dominate the campus environment, thus creating a strong institutional "press" for student impact. Institutions with the most powerful effects on their graduates are those where the student and faculty goals and values are similar.

## Residential and Commuter Campuses

Another institutional variable that can make a significant difference to students is the degree of "residentialness" at a given college or university. Virtually every analysis of this topic concludes that the effects of college are greatly enhanced by living on campus (Kent and Astin 1983; Astin 1977; Bowen 1977; Chickering and Kuper 1971; Chickering 1974; Feldman and Newcomb 1969; Schuster and Coil 1982; Winter et al. 1981). The results of Winter et al. even suggest that a student who does not live on campus, but who attends a residential college, is influenced more by the collegiate experience than is a student who attends a commuter campus.

Chickering devoted an entire study to the differences between residential students and commuting students. His results show that, even after controlling for the background characteristics of matriculants at entrance, residential students have more contact with faculty, are more likely to persist, are less likely to fail a course or be on academic probation, spend less time watching TV, have higher aspirations, are more self-confident, and are more likely to be involved in campus activities. Feldman and Newcomb demonstrate that residential students tend to be better adjusted socially and that men are usually more satisfied with mixed-sex housing, while women tend to be more satisfied with single-sex housing. Schuster and Coil write that commuters generally perceive themselves to be less popular and have fewer close friends. In summary, attending a residential college or university does make a difference in student development. Whatever the overall impact of a particular institution, that impact is accentuated by the residential quality of the institution. The principal reason for this appears to be that students at residential institutions are more likely to become involved in the academic and social life of the campus.

## Institutional Selectivity

The degree of selectivity also has some effect on students. Astin (1977) reports a positive relationship between the selectivity of the institution and student satisfaction. Students attending such colleges are more apt to describe the environment as exerting "strong pressures for academic performance" (p. 179). It also appears that more selective institutions encourage greater spontaneity and coping skills (p. 179). Schuster and Coil (1982) note that high-quality liberal arts colleges seem to do a better job of facilitating the development of the whole student.

Feldman and Newcomb (1969) conclude that schools with the highest intellectual rankings produce the lowest gain scores in intellectual orientation. Conversely, students at colleges of lower status produce greater gain scores. Nevertheless, although the gap between the scores at the two types of institutions has been narrowed, students at the more selective campuses still maintain their lead (p. 141).

Astin, in his thorough work, notes that students attending selective institutions show larger-than-average declines in religion, larger increases in self-criticism, and lower grade point averages (but do not have lower self-concepts in intellectual self-esteem). In addition, they are less likely than the average student to demonstrate, drink, or get married while in college. One area that does not appear to be affected by selectivity is the academic achievement of students. This seems to be related more to the matriculant's ability at entrance. Schuster and Coil write that "despite a wide variety of approaches, the relationship between academic achievement and institutional quality appears to be negligible" (p. 55). As mentioned above in the section on leadership, Winter et al. (1981) assert that more selective colleges and universities engender a sense of "specialness" that is related to self-esteem and leadership motivation. This concept of specialness best characterizes the effects of selectivity. Students know they are in an environment that is more selective, thus gaining greater satisfaction and a more positive self-image.

## Religiously Affiliated Colleges and Universities

Religious institutions of higher education seem to have a different set of effects on their students than do nonreligious institutions. Although the religious beliefs and activities of most students decline during their college years, Astin (1977) finds that going to a Protestant or Roman Catholic college reduces the amount of decline. He states that attending sectarian institutions encourages the development of altruism among students, and there tends to be a greater satisfaction with student-faculty relationships. Similarly, Schuster and Coil (1982) note that students at such schools are more satisfied with the sense of community and student friendships. Also, Astin says, hedonism scores are not as high at religiously affiliated colleges.

Trent (in Feldman and Newcomb 1969) notes that Roman Catholic students attending Roman Catholic colleges have higher scores on scales of authoritarianism. Pace (1972) reports that religious institutions that place a strong emphasis on control and propriety produce students who are less open and less tolerant. Feldman and Newcomb document an inverse relationship between religious orthodoxy and authoritarianism and dogmatism. This suggests that sectarian institutions may encourage greater religious orthodoxy and attitudes, but they also provide a setting in which students are not so likely to develop open and tolerant values.

The impact of religiously affiliated colleges and universities thus is a mixed picture. These colleges seem to be more likely to produce graduates who hold to the values of the sponsoring organization, but may also graduate students who are more authoritarian and dogmatic.

## Single Sex and Coeducation

The past two decades have seen many single-sex colleges shift to coeducation in the belief that this would bolster enrollments and improve the overall quality of the educational environment. The results of research on this topic, however, raise many questions regarding the wisdom of these changes.

Attending single-sex colleges increases the chances of becoming involved in academic activities, having more contact with faculty, and being verbally aggressive (Astin 1977). Astin also documents an increase in the likelihood of being in an honors program and participating in intercollegiate athletics. Kent and Astin (1983) find that women who assume leadership positions on a campus are more likely to develop a greater sense of self-confidence and have an interest in taking on leadership roles after graduation. There is a greater probability that women will fill such roles at a single-sex college.

Schuster and Coil (1982) state that women attending women's colleges will be more likely to develop higher aspirations and complete their college education. They also write that there is a greater probability that students will be satisfied with "all aspects of the undergraduate experience, except social life . . ." (p. 51). The evidence indicates that the benefits of enrolling in single-sex colleges are many and positive.

## Size

Institutional size has also been found to have an effect on the lives of college students. Size interacts with many of the institutional variables already discussed in this section. Wilson and Gaff (1975) found that students had more frequent contact with faculty at smaller colleges. Their results indicated that students at larger schools had to be more aggressive in seeking out discussions with faculty. In almost every area of college life, students show less involvement at larger campuses (Astin 1977; Feldman and Newcomb 1969; Schuster and Coil 1982). Astin reveals fewer opportunities for leadership, lessened development of altruism, and mixed results in student satisfaction. Similarly, Feldman and Newcomb state that size has a negative impact on self-ratings of popularity.

Students at larger universities are generally more dissatisfied with both the level of instruction and the relationships with faculty. On the other hand, they are usually more satisfied with the curriculum, the reputation of the institution, and the social life of the campus (Schuster and Coil). Astin also reports that students at larger universities are more likely to graduate with honors.

Despite the seemingly positive results from going to a small college, Feldman and Newcomb conclude that it still remains unclear whether it is better to be a "big frog in a small pond or a small frog in a big pond" (p. 239). There are definite benefits in attending both types of institution. It would appear, however, that smaller colleges generally offer a more positive environment for matriculants.

## MEASURING COLLEGE IMPACT

In one sense everything that has preceded this portion of Chapter 7 is intended to encourage enrollment managers to ascertain the impact their individual institutions have on their students. The research cited up to this point may help enrollment managers to justify students' enrolling in a specific institution, but only an in-house research program can actually validate the effects of a specific campus.

Many surveys and questionnaires that have been developed and tested for reliability and validity are available. Baird, Hartnett, and Associates provide a comprehensive review of the variety of instruments available to assess the noncognitive effects of college in their book titled *Understanding Student and Faculty Life* (1980). They describe and give usage examples of instruments that can assess campus environments, measure the degree of student satisfaction with college, and determine institutional goals as perceived by students and faculty.

The College Board, in conjunction with the National Center for Higher Education Management Systems, offers a series of questionnaires designed to assess student attitudes and characteristics upon entrance: The entering Student Questionnaire and the Continuing Student Questionnaire. These examine the goals and satisfaction of current students and are available for both two- and four-year colleges. The set of survey instruments also includes a completer or graduate questionnaire. The American College Testing Program also has developed a survey, The Student Opinion Survey, which looks at satisfaction and attitudes of current students.

Pace has recently developed a research instrument designed to measure the energy and effort a student puts forth in using the human and physical resources of an individual college or university. It attempts to measure the quality of student effort. Although the instrument is too new to be described in any detail, the concept is an intriguing one, given the relationship established in this chapter between involvement and impact. The instrument, The College Student Experience, is available through the Higher Education Research Institute in Los Angeles.

In addition to the noncognitive effects of college, the cognitive dimension should be examined as well. Both Educational Testing Service (ETS) and the American College Testing Program (ACT) have recently developed instruments to measure general cognitive learning in undergraduate programs. The ACT program, called COMP (College Outcome Measures Project), attempts to measure the skills students gain that will assist them in functioning in the world. It looks at communication, problem solving, values clarification, the ability to function within social institutions, the ability to use science and technology, and the use of the arts. The ETS program, the Undergraduate Assessment Program, assesses cognitive growth in four areas: humanities, natural sciences, social sciences, and aptitude. In addition, colleges have undertaken such tasks as comparing SAT or ACT scores at entrance with GRE scores at graduation, comparing the student's overall percentile scores. Self-appraisals, using current students and/or alumni, have also been utilized to determine cognitive growth.

In addition to all of the packaged tools available, Brown presents a detailed outline for assessing the effects of higher education (see *The Outputs of Higher Education: Their Identification, Measurement, and Evalua-*

*tion,* Chapter 2, "A Scheme for Measuring the Output of Higher Education," 1970). Brown presents a step-by-step plan for measuring the impact and outcomes of higher education. His methodologies often include student self-report and self-appraisal forms that can be developed on individual campuses. Brown makes the point that even simple measurement techniques can be informative and are far superior to no information.

## AN APPRAISAL OF THE EFFECTS OF COLLEGE ON STUDENTS

Colleges and universities do appear to have an effect on the lives of the students that attend them. These effects vary according to the type of institution attended as well as the characteristics of the entering matriculants. Furthermore, the impact of college is mediated by the level of student involvement and experiences.

It is little wonder that social scientists have chosen to be cautious in reporting the results of their research on this topic. They use verbs such as appears, seems, is likely, tend to—in this literature. For the most part, this is necessary. Whether colleges really change students or whether factors of student maturation and student disposition account for much of the development is difficult to determine in some areas.

On the whole, with the development of more sophisticated research methodologies, considerations of maturation and disposition can in many instances be controlled. It may be concluded that pursuing a college degree does lead to the development of a broad general knowledge base and a specialized reservoir of information.

In noncognitive growth, most students do become more open and tolerant, more self-confident, more mature and adaptable, more able to critically evaluate situations, and more likely to get involved with the society in which they live. While the exact nature and degree of change in college students is not always ascertainable, the general direction of change is. College does have an impact on students: For many it does make a difference in their lives; for most it is a wise consumptive investment.

## SUGGESTIONS FOR FURTHER READING

*Four Critical Years,* by Alexander Astin.
*Investment in Learning: Individual and Social Value of American Education,* by Howard Bowen.

*The Impact of College on Students*, vol. 1, by Kenneth Feldman and Theodore Newcomb.

*Measuring the Outcomes of College: Fifty Years of Findings and Recommendations for the Future*, by C. Robert Pace.

"The Effects of Type of College on Students," by Jack Schuster and Ann Coil. In W. Lowery and Associates (eds.), *College Admissions Counseling*.

# Chapter 8

# The Outcomes of Higher Education

## THE SIGNIFICANCE OF HIGHER EDUCATION OVER A LIFETIME

The introduction to Chapters 7 and 8 examined the distinction between the impact and the outcomes of higher education. This chapter explores the outcomes of obtaining a college degree. While the evidence supports the conclusion that college attendance does have an effect on college students, there is perhaps an even more important question: What are the lasting and enduring effects of going to college? Does college make a difference over the lifetime of graduates? In addition, since most institutions, even private ones, are subsidized to some degree by the public, do institutions of higher education have an impact on society at large? These questions are often referred to as the "benefits question." What are the benefits of higher education—to the individual consumer as well as to society?

For enrollment managers such questions are not entirely academic. Students and parents are interested in how the graduates will fare after college. Will they be able to get good jobs? Will they earn a good living? What kind of life-styles are they likely to enjoy? In many public arenas, it is the college president and often those in admissions and recruitment who are being asked to articulate the benefits of higher education to public policymakers. They are increasingly called upon to justify the public investment in higher education. Thus, it behooves enrollment managers to become more familiar with this important area of research.

The primary focus of this chapter is on the economic and noneconomic benefits, or outcomes, of higher education. From this perspective the economic, or pecuniary, benefits of college for the student consumers are explored as well as the economic benefits that accrue to society. Some societal outcomes, however, are nonpecuniary; these are also presented.

Before we begin the review of the literature on outcomes, two issues need to be discussed. One question that often emerges is whether the changes that occur in college actually persist. The other issue is ability versus education: Does innate ability make a greater difference in lifetime earning patterns and the kinds of jobs procured, or does education play a more important role?

With regard to the persistence of college impact, Chapter 7 should be reconsidered for a moment. Although the years spent in college do have an impact on students, the persistence of these changes was not addressed. The degree to which the effects of college endure over a lifetime was not examined. If the impact of college does not persist, the significance of the college experience is greatly diminished. As will be seen in the discussion of the noneconomic benefits of higher education, the impact of college does carry over into later life in many areas—such as flexibility and tolerance, political attitudes, aspirations, and cultural interests. Only in the areas of hedonism and religious activities does the impact of college seem to diminish. Although college graduates continue to be less orthodox in their religious values, church attendance patterns and other indicators of religion do increase after graduation. The hedonistic behavior of college graduates declines (Astin 1977). For the most part, virtually all studies that examine this issue have concluded that the effects of college persist (Astin 1977; Bowen 1977; Feldman and Newcomb 1969; Ramist 1981; Solmon and Oschner 1978; Whithey 1971).

As to the relative importance of education or ability, this question has been examined most thoroughly by Jencks el al. (1977). They review several large studies that compared the career paths and earning streams, or patterns, of brothers and twin brothers. (This population was chosen because family background characteristics were less likely to be confounding variables.) Jencks estimates that a college degree accounts for 30 to 40 percent of the earnings differential between high school and college graduates when all background variables are controlled (p. 188). On college attendance versus college completion, he notes that the first year of college and the graduation year raise earnings twice as much as do the intervening years (p. 227). Although the finding is not directly related to this point, Jencks also asserts that for students of similar ability, college selectivity has no effect on the status of the job the student enters after college, but it does positively affect the eventual income level (p. 186). Jencks concludes: "The best readily observable predictor of a young man's eventual status or earnings is the amount of schooling he has had" (p. 230). With this background, the outcomes of higher education will be presented.

## THE INDIVIDUAL ECONOMIC BENEFITS OF HIGHER EDUCATION

Most discussions regarding the individual economic, or pecuniary, benefits of college attendance center around the issue of the rate of return. That is, how much more do college attenders earn than do non–college attenders? The economic benefits of higher education are much broader, however, than simply the rate of return. Fringe benefits, mobility, and employability are also part of the pecuniary benefits issue.

## The Rate of Return

In the early 1970s a number of economists and social critics suggested that a college degree may no longer be the good investment that it once was (Bird 1975; Freeman 1976; Hapgood 1971). The questions raised by these criticisms have persisted in the minds of many people, including prospective students, parents, high school counselors, and public policymakers. These critics suggest that as the result of slowed economic growth, diplomaism, and the overproduction of college degree holders, higher education is no longer providing a good rate of return. Bird states that high school graduates would receive a higher rate of return if they went to work immediately and invested the money they would have spent on college.

To be sure, the rate of return has declined over the past two decades. In 1958 Kiker (1971) estimated that the average high school graduate earned $135,000 compared with $258,000 for a college graduate (p. 175). Becker (in Eckaus, Safty, and Norman 1975, p. 341) determined that the individual return for a college education in the 1950s was 14.5 percent. More recent studies have projected rates of return of 4 to 11 percent (Douglas 1977; Freeman 1975; Perlman 1973; Taubman and Wales 1973), which represents a significant decline. Part of this decline, however, is the result of more sophisticated research methodologies.

A simple comparison of the annual or lifetime earnings of high school and college graduates does not take into consideration that the "average" high school graduate is not so capable as the comparable college degree holder, nor are high school and college graduates as likely to come from the same socioeconomic background. Very early studies also did not account for the costs of higher education—both the direct costs and the opportunity costs. This partially explains the apparent decline in the rate of return. Nevertheless, it has declined.

As early as 1949, Harris (in Berg 1970, p. 45) warned that America might be producing more college graduates than could be absorbed into the occupations they would expect to fill. From 1964 to 1974, the growth in occupations of college-intensive industries did not keep up with the growth of holders of college degrees (Berg 1970; Freeman 1976). As a result, college graduates have experienced underemployment and have accepted jobs in areas of lesser status (Berg 1970; Freeman 1976; Hapgood 1971; Thurow 1974).

On the other hand, Gordon and Alhadeff (1980) point out that looking at the 1960s may not be a fair basis of comparison. They believe that the decline may be exaggerated because of the booming employment market for college graduates during the 1960s. The reports of increased numbers of college graduates accepting blue-collar jobs since 1960 is accurate; however, comparisons with the 1950s reveal a pattern similar to the current one (see Figure 12).

In addition, it is important to note that over 75 percent of all college graduates are employed in professional and managerial positions (p. 187). In constant dollars the rate of return did decline between 1969 and 1977. On the other hand, the rate of return in 1977 was almost equal to that of the year 1959 and well above the rate in 1949 (p. 182). Thus, it appears that the decade of the 1960s was an aberrant period for the economic benefits of higher education as well as for political and social values. Any data that compare the 1960s and the 1970s may not be presenting an accurate picture of higher education's economic benefits.

## Employability and Fringe Benefits

The fringe benefits of employment are also part of the economic benefits of going to college. Just as white-collar jobs have tended to pay better salaries, they usually have better job security and fringe benefits (Hossler 1979). White-collar workers are seldom subject to seasonal unemployment or strikes; they are also able to have longer careers than are blue-collar workers (Bowen 1977). As noted in Chapter 2 in the section on Rate of Return, recent college graduates are three times less likely to experience unemployment. Froomkin (1980) finds that college graduates have less difficulty finding jobs. Professionals and other white-collar workers are more likely to have better fringe benefits such as health programs, life insurance, and vacation privileges (Spady 1967). Pascharopoulus (1975) reports that the calculated rates of return would rise by one-fifth if paid holidays and vacation alone were taken into consideration (pp. 134–61).

## Mobility

College graduates generally find it easier to move from one job to another and to advance within their chosen occupation. Beaton (1975) and Strumpel (in Kiker 1971), note that college degree holders are more likely than non–degree holders to rate their chances good for advancement at the workplace. College graduates are more able to change jobs and do so more often (Jencks et al. 1977). A consortium of five Michigan institutions conducting a follow-up study of their alumni in nontraditional programs

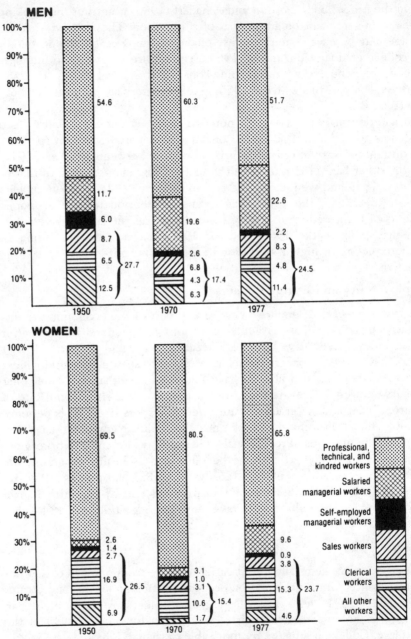

**Figure** 12 Occupational distribution of college graduates: 1950, 1970, 1977.

report that many of their graduates also experience increased incomes and job mobility. Furthermore, Bowen (1977) writes that college graduates are more open to career changes and are more willing to make geographic relocations to take advantage of job advancements. They are more versatile and better able to learn on the job. College degree holders are generally more in control of their career "portfolio" and have more allocative ability in the labor market (Bowen 1977; Freeman 1971; Juster 1975; Strumpel 1971).

### Individual Pecuniary Benefits and the Future

Research generally supports the notion that a college degree does pay—it appears to be "worth it." Gordon and Alhadeff (1980) have determined that the rate of return has not changed substantially since 1973 (p. 188). Rumberger (1982) asserts that "even though an increasing number of college graduates are now finding it difficult to find jobs commensurate with their level of training, an individual is still more likely to find a good job with a college degree than with a high school diploma" (p. 461). In addition, there is good reason to believe that in the late 1980s, because of the reduced number of college graduates and the increased number of retirements from the labor force, the employment market and thus the rate of return will begin to climb again for degree holders.

## THE INDIVIDUAL NONECONOMIC BENEFITS OF HIGHER EDUCATION

Just as there are individual economic benefits that are derived from college attendance, there are noneconomic outcomes as well. These include such benefits as greater happiness, mental health, increased tolerance, and improved child-rearing habits. The nonpecuniary benefits are not so easily quantified as the pecuniary benefits, but for many college graduates they are no less important than the economic outcomes.

### Intellectual, Cultural, and Social Benefits

College graduates generally believe that their college provided them with a somewhat good or a good background for their vocational life (Pace 1979, p. 100). Pace also reports that very few college alumni have negative feelings about their college experience. College alumni typically find their work more enjoyable, challenging, and interesting (Beaton 1975). In addition, they tend to save more money and are wiser consumers (Bowen 1977).

With regard to cultural and intellectual activities, college degree holders are more likely to read books and magazines, attend plays and concerts, and go to museums (Pace 1979; Spaeth and Greely 1970; Whithey 1971). College graduates spend less time watching TV and make more constructive use of their leisure time (Pace 1979; Bowen 1977). They report that college has helped them to think more analytically and critically, as well as to explain themselves more effectively.

One of the few studies looking at the alumni of nontraditional programs was conducted by a consortium of five Michigan institutions. The group included public and private as well as two- and four-year colleges and universities. The study concludes there are few differences in terms of satisfaction, broadened reading interests, and increased interest in political issues between traditional and nontraditional students. The authors do report greater vocational interests among nontraditional-age students.

The outcomes discussed in this section cover a wide spectrum of activities and are not inconsequential. The happiness and satisfaction of individuals and their families cannot readily be measured, but are nevertheless invaluable outcomes of college and university experience.

## Health and the Family

College graduates seem to be healthier in every sense. They are less likely to miss work because of illness, are able to work until a later age, and experience a lower incidence of mental illness when compared with high school graduates (Bowen 1977; Juster 1975; Whithey 1971). They report being happier and more satisfied with life (Bowen 1977). After interviewing 2,460 persons over 21 years of age, Gurin, Veroff, and Feldman (in Bowen 1977) reached the following conclusions about college graduates:

> First, people with more education seem to be more introspective about themselves, more concerned about personal and interpersonal aspects of their lives. Secondly, more educated people seem to have coupled with their introspectiveness a greater sense of well-being and satisfaction. . . . The more highly educated respondents . . . seem to be more aware of both the positive and negative aspects of their lives. They are happier in their overall evaluation of their current happiness, in their marriages, and in their jobs—and more optimistic about the future than the less educated respondents (p. 116).

College graduates also appear to have better child-rearing practices. College-educated parents spend more time with their children on nonphysical needs (Leibowitz 1975). This is true for both parents but particularly for mothers. Parents with college degrees spend a larger percentage of their income on education and related activities. As a result, it is not surprising to discover that the sons and daughters of college-educated parents are more likely to go to college themselves (Bowen 1977). This intergenerational transmission of education is an important outcome of attending college.

Here again, the outcomes of going to college are positive. It is difficult to attach an economic value to the health and the well-being of a family. Nevertheless, few would argue that these are inconsequential benefits of higher education.

## THE CONSUMPTIVE BENEFITS OF HIGHER EDUCATION

Not only do students receive many benefits from colleges and universities in later life, they receive benefits while attending. These rewards are commonly referred to as the consumptive benefits of higher education—those activities students find rewarding and pleasurable while "consuming" higher education. The consumptive benefits can range from having ready access to athletic contests and cultural activities to going to dances and films. Consumptive benefits include being in a setting where there are large numbers of people who are at a similar stage of development with somewhat similar interests. These benefits can include the satisfaction of gaining new knowledge, making new friends, or finding a spouse. Many college alumni would repeat the college experience just for the consumptive benefits.

### The Consumptive Rate of Return

Any review of outcomes that ignores the consumptive benefits of higher education runs the risk of overlooking an important return on the investment in a college degree. In fact, Adkins (1975) suggests that if the fringe, noneconomic, and consumptive benefits were accurately quantified and taken into consideration, the rate of return would look quite different. He asserts that rather than a 4 to 11 percent rate of return, the rate would be between 40 and 50 percent (p. 176). The true rate of return is difficult to ascertain. It is much easier to derive a return rate that takes into consideration only wages, the opportunity cost, and the direct costs of higher education. The noneconomic and consumptive benefits, however, complicate the rate-of-return equation; yet they can be an important part of the benefits of going to college.

## THE ECONOMIC SOCIETAL OUTCOMES
## OF HIGHER EDUCATION

For many years higher education has been viewed as a positive influence in the growth of the nation's productivity. Schultz (1963) attributes 16.5

to 20 percent of the growth in the GNP to higher education (p. 45). Dennison (1971) arrives at similar figures. According to Wykstra (1971), one reason for the large contribution of higher education is that the return on education is much greater in countries that are technologically advanced.

The economic contributions of higher education to society can be understood in two ways. First, college degree holders, as discussed in Chapters 7 and 8, are more adaptable and learn more quickly on the job, thus contributing to efficiency and productivity. Wykstra supports this conclusion: "Highly educated people make good innovators, so that education speeds the process of technological diffusion" (p. 95). Second, the research capabilities of colleges and universities themselves have made possible important discoveries in applied and basic research that have led to new inventions and new technological advancements. Rosenzweig (1982), for example, believes that current developments in genetic splicing and recombinant DNA are the direct result of over 20 years of basic research in genetics, organic chemistry, and molecular biology. He states no one could have predicted this when the work first began. Investigators such as Rosenzweig are currently attempting to make a case that the federal government is not investing enough in higher education to assure that similar unforeseen developments will take place 20 years from today.

Society also benefits from the individual contributions of college degree holders. College graduates save more money and make wiser investments (Bowen 1977). They pay more taxes and are less likely to be a drain on society via unemployment or disability payments. In large and small ways college contributes to the economic wealth and vitality of the nation.

## THE NONECONOMIC SOCIETAL OUTCOMES OF HIGHER EDUCATION

The nonpecuniary benefits of higher education to society are many and varied. Holders of college degrees vote more often than others and have a greater tendency to become involved in political issues at all levels of government (Bowen 1977; Pace 1979; Spaeth and Greely 1970). Over two-thirds of all college graduates believe that the collegiate experience helped them to develop greater social competence and enhanced their ability to get along with different types of people (Pace, pp. 104–105). Bowen concludes that college alumni also tend to hold more liberal views in such areas as civil liberties, individual freedom, discrimination, political activism, taxes, and government expenditures. Most studies also suggest that college graduates have a broader base of knowledge and can therefore better understand the changes and events in our society (Bowen 1977; Pace 1979; Spaeth and Greely 1970; Whithey 1971).

If Jencks et al. (1977) are correct that higher education is the best predictor of occupational status and, to a lesser degree, income, colleges and universities have played and can continue to play an important role in advancing social equality in this country. As Bowen suggests, a country that espouses democratic ideals requires an involved and educated citizenry in order to function at its highest level. Furthermore, a democratic society is built on the principles of equality in all areas, including the equality of opportunity.

## THE BENEFITS QUESTION

At this point the relevance of research on college choice may seem far more practical and appropriate for administrators who seek to manage enrollments. In a most direct way, perhaps they are more useful. Nevertheless, marketing within an enrollment management context requires that college and university spokespersons be able to articulate the benefits of going to college to prospective matriculants, parents, and public policy-makers. These spokespersons must be able to build a case for supporting specific institutions of higher learning. This overview of the outcomes of a college education, coupled with the discussion in Chapter 7 of the impact of college on students, provides the necessary perspective.

In summary, Pace (1979) has written a simple yet thorough analysis of the outcomes of higher education:

—Do college graduates have good jobs? Yes.
—Do college graduates have good incomes? Yes.
—Do college graduates like their jobs? Yes.
—Do college graduates think their education was relevant to their jobs? Yes.
—Do college graduates feel satisfied about the colleges they attended? Yes.
—Do college graduates think their education developed their ability to think critically and express themselves clearly? Yes.
—Do college graduates think their education gave them breadth of knowledge about various fields? Yes.
—Do college graduates think their education helped them in understanding and relating to other people? Yes.
—Do college graduates think their education helped them to develop and clarify their goals and values? Yes (pp. 105–106).

## MEASURING THE OUTCOMES

To clearly document the outcomes of specific institutions, enrollment managers will need to organize the institutional research efforts. Feedback from the alumni can be an invaluable source of information. Institutions have to keep track of their alumni—what they do and how they feel about their alma mater. Martorana (in Baird 1977) states that former students can be an excellent source of information about the institution.

The College Board, in conjunction with the National Center for Higher Education Management Systems, publishes questionnaires for recent and long-term alumni. The American College Testing Program also has an alumni survey that is available. In addition, some of the assessment procedures suggested by Brown (1970) are relevant to outcomes measurement. There are no published instruments, however, that will provide information on all the issues discussed in this chapter. In all likelihood, colleges and universities will find it necessary to develop some of their own instruments. The career placement office and the alumni office can be helpful in gathering data about the employment history and earning streams of former students.

An area often overlooked for analysis is the impact an institution of higher learning has on its local community. This is particularly relevant for community colleges, which are funded by local taxing districts. The study recently published in the *Community and Junior College Journal* (McCuen 1983) is a good example of how a college can articulate the benefits of a college campus to a community (pp. 20–21).

The more enrollment managers can document impact and outcomes as they relate to their specific institution, the more effectively they will be able to market their institution to the various constituencies of the college or university. This brings the enrollment manager full cycle with a return to the initial phases of the college-choice process—influencing choice through effective institutional communication efforts.

The research that can provide a perspective for enrollment managers is diverse, ranging from the economics of higher education to sociological studies of college choice and college impact. This perspective will not always lead directly to new activities or more effective programs, but at times it will, and it will always provide the basis for more informed decision making. Schuster and Coil (1982) speak to this: "Paradoxically, probably less and less use of evidence about student development is being made today in formulating institutional policies for recruiting students. . . . To the best of our knowledge, administrators and college faculty are virtually illiterate when it comes to understanding the multidimensional effects of colleges on students" (pp. 74–75). Finally, familiarity with this knowledge base and the ability to use it can provide the foundation for the professionalization of the admissions function.

## SUGGESTIONS FOR FURTHER READING

*Investment in Learning: Individual and Social Value of American Higher Education*, by Howard Bowen.
*The Over-Educated American*, by Richard Freeman.

## Chapter 9

# Toward Enrollment Management

## DESIGNING AN ENROLLMENT MANAGEMENT PLAN

An effective plan for managing enrollments encompasses a wide-ranging set of activities. From planning for demand and developing marketing and recruitment strategies to following the careers and personal lives of alumni, managing collegiate enrollments includes many diverse elements (Figure 13). Enrollment managers may not always have direct control over all of these activities; nevertheless, they should have a sense of the important questions to be asked and understand the nature of the tasks an institution should undertake if it is to exert a stronger influence on the size, shape, and quality of its student body.

### Planning for Demand

An enrollment management process begins with strategic planning that outlines the desired characteristics of the student body and the activities the institution will engage in to attract and retain such students. This planning process should address a realistic assessment of the demand for the college's product. It should involve careful enrollment projections, which begin with a conservative base. It is much easier for an institution to adjust its revenue projections upward after a successful recruitment campaign than it is to reduce the revenue estimates after an overly optimistic projection. These projections should take into consideration past enrollment trends as well as demand features such as the economy, labor market, direction of public policy, and demographic trends.

Many large colleges and universities have developed computer software programs that permit them to make sophisticated enrollment projections. Stanford University, for instance, has a highly developed system that integrates enrollment projections and budgetary factors. EDUCOM markets an enrollment projection software program that can be used on microcom-

**Figure** 13 An enrollment management system.

puters. Wing (1980) provides a thorough discussion of enrollment planning in *Improving Academic Management: A Handbook of Planning and Institutional Research*.

## Influencing College Choice

The topic that probably needs the least emphasis is influencing college choice. This area is typically the domain of admissions personnel. Enrollment managers will need to analyze carefully the factors that affect choice at their institutions. They will also have to take into account the complexity of the choice process and to understand that it is the culmination of a long developmental process. No single marketing technique or new program is likely to resolve the enrollment concerns of a college or university.

One area that needs greater attention is competitive assessment. Too many enrollment managers cannot identify their competition with any degree of confidence. Most administrators are even less sure of why students chose a specific institution from a competitive set. Decision makers who lack an adequate understanding of their campus image and how they compare with other institutions (as well as noneducational options in the case of community colleges) may not take advantage of important opportunities. Conversely, it is equally possible that administrators will take inappropriate actions based on faulty perceptions. Although the notion of competitive assessment still carries negative connotations to many within the academy, it can enhance institutional self-understanding. Quality and uniqueness combined with flexibility, sound leadership, and the ability to identify and serve student markets are important dimensions of an enrollment management system.

## Pricing: Finding the Right Niche

In an era of competition among colleges and universities, the cost of purchasing the product, as with all industries, is the point at which much of the competition may take place. This price competition is not likely to result in actual price wars in many locations. Institutions of higher learning, however, are already engaged in more subtle forms of cost competition. Marketing techniques designed to communicate net price as opposed to list price; the mix of scholarships, grants, loans, and work-study; and the increase in no-need financial aid are all forms of such competition.

Lacking at many institutions is a clear notion of how their pricing policies actually affect the choice decision. Most colleges are not sure how their financial aid packages influence the nature of the student body and are even less sure how their awards compare with those of their competition. This returns to the idea of competitive assessment. There is a great need for institutional research in this area on each campus. Unlike some of the software packages available for enrollment projections, packaged resources are not readily available for competitive assessment. This is a critical topic for further research.

## Recruiting Graduates

Student-institution fit is a less tangible quality than some of the other factors discussed in this work; yet it is no less important. Enrollment managers should try to develop a sense of the qualities of the campuses at which they are employed. No instrument can accurately identify all the characteristics of a campus environment, thus predicting the degree of fit for each potential matriculant. Yet every campus has its own unique personality—a milieu—which characterizes the institution. The more successfully managers of enrollment can understand the uniqueness of their individual campus environments, the more successful they will be in recruiting graduates.

## Implementing an Attrition-Alert System

Retaining students has become an increasingly important aspect of an enrollment management system. There are two elements of a sound retention program. First, enrollment managers must have a firm grasp of the increasingly large body of research on student retention. This provides the basis for the development of the second element of an effective retention system.

Programs designed to reduce student attrition are the second part of such a system. These programs must begin with the identification of potential dropouts and should be followed by the marketing of the programs to target populations. For this to be effective, it is necessary to assign the administrative responsibilities for such a program to one administrator who can both evaluate the effectiveness of retention activities and work effectively with all campus segments—students, faculty, and administrators.

## Completing the Cycle: Research and Evaluation

Despite the importance of all the areas discussed thus far, the most crucial elements, perhaps, of any enrollment system are a quality institutional research effort and thorough program evaluation. Without these two components it will be difficult, if not impossible, for enrollment managers to have access to the kind of data necessary to make informed decisions in marketing, financial aid awards, and retention efforts.

The importance of program evaluation and institutional research is the foundation of this book. For many institutions with scarce resources, who cannot afford well-staffed offices in these two areas, the prospects of an effective enrollment management operation may seem dim. The sophistication of these activities can vary, however, and still produce useful results. Large campuses will often have the resources to organize strong research and evaluation programs, but small campuses, too, can set up these programs.

At campuses with fewer resources, these activities can be carried out on a decentralized basis. As part of the planning process, the dean or vice-president of enrollment management can prepare enrollment projections. The admissions office, perhaps in conjunction with the development office, can conduct marketing research. In addition, the admissions office can conduct an analysis of the competition. The financial aid office can be responsible for gathering data on financial aid awards and developing a pricing and marketing plan to maximize the use of scarce dollars. The student affairs office can work with areas such as orientation, athletics, residence life, and the student retention program. They can also conduct research, design activities, and evaluate them. The alumni office and the career placement office can assist with the alumni surveys—tracking the career paths and the earning streams of former students. A decentralized system may not work so effectively as an office staffed by well-trained professionals, but it can still provide information that can be invaluable for an enrollment management system. For such a system to work, a senior-level administrator with the authority to coordinate all the above activities is required. If this is not possible, the president will have to function in this role and must know enough about enrollment management to work effectively in this capacity.

At schools with centralized institutional research offices, new priorities may need to be established. A problem that can occur on many campuses is the failure of such offices to conduct studies that can easily be applied to actual situations. More often, senior-level administrators do not set the agenda for institutional researchers, leaving them to complete Higher Education General Information Survey (HEGIS) reports and to conduct space utilization studies. The task for enrollment managers is to play a key role in setting the agenda for research offices and to know what to do with the information after it is collected.

Although it is not within the scope of this work, one other area should be addressed. The importance of a management information system cannot be overlooked. Both institutional research efforts and successful marketing activities depend on computer systems that permit the easy storage, manipulation, and access of information. With the development of microcomputers and their increasing ability to interface with mainframe systems, this is within the reach of almost any college or university. It is difficult to conceive of a successful enrollment management plan that does not include a management information system.

## THE LIMITATIONS OF ENROLLMENT MANAGEMENT

### The Potential

An enrollment management approach to marketing, recruitment, and retention activities offers the possibility of a more effective approach to shaping collegiate enrollments—to attracting students with the characteristics and qualities to thrive and flourish at the college or university of their choice. It also offers the hope of a more satisfying match of student and institution.

Well-conceptualized plans to manage enrollments can lead to a better institutional self-understanding and an enhanced institutional health and vitality. With adequate information about the institutional environment and sufficient data about the actual and potential markets of a college or university, enrollment managers may indeed be able to influence college choice effectively. Kemerer, Baldridge, and Green (1982) provide examples of successful enrollment management programs. Muston (1984), in a recent study of Midwestern state universities, presents the persuasive evidence that enrollment management systems can work. Whereas Kemerer, Baldridge, and Green use the case study approach, Muston, using American College Testing Program data, finds a significant positive relationship between those institutions with enrollment management systems and those who have experienced increases in the quality of their entering classes. These universities have also attracted increasing numbers of entering students. Muston concludes that "those institutions with centrally coordinated enrollment management plans and strategies experienced measurable gains in their undergraduate enrollment status during a four-year period" (p. 26).

Despite the promising findings of Kemerer, Baldridge, and Green and Muston, there is the possibility that the concept of enrollment management will be oversold or abused. It is always possible that increased knowledge about the college-choice process and market-sensitive pricing can be manipulated. In the short run, enrollment managers may devise new techniques that will increase enrollments quickly by manipulating some of the choice variables. Nevertheless, in the long run, poor student-institution fit and the lack of student satisfaction with the campus environment can only harm the college's marketing and recruitment efforts. Enrollment management programs built on poor information or unethical practices will result in eventual failure and can potentially not only harm the image of the specific campus, but diminish the respect for our entire system of higher education. Unethical or poorly organized enrollment management plans can serve to strengthen the hold of consumerism on colleges and universities.

Consumerism has been healthy for colleges and universities in the United States in many ways. It has forced colleges to greater levels of accountability. It has reminded some institutions that a primary function they perform is educating and responding to the needs of students. Nevertheless, an overemphasis on consumerism can do damage to the academy. College students do not always know what is best for them. The liberalizing experience of the general education programs has some positive benefits for students and for society. A healthy tension between consumerism in higher education and the ability of institutions to stand independently—to in fact retain some remnant of that battered image of the ivory tower—is necessary. Misguided enrollment management plans can disrupt this delicate tension.

Of less significance, but not lacking in importance, is the potential for the concept of enrollment management to be oversold. The adoption of an enrollment management system will not be a panacea for institutions of higher education. Boards of trustees, college presidents, and faculty members will have to come to grips with the realities of their particular situation.

For a rural residential college in the Midwest, an enrollment manager may be very successful if student enrollments do not fall by more than 10 percent. A less selective commuter college in the Northeast may have a strong program if enrollments hold steady. A community college in the West may have a weak enrollment management effort if enrollments remain constant. A realistic assessment of the competitive environment in which an institution functions is a critical element of strategic planning and the reference point for evaluating the effectiveness of any enrollment management plan. It is essential that college presidents operate from an informed perspective.

## Enrollment Managers

One of the key questions that emerge from this discussion of enrollment management for those institutions that wish to adopt such a model is: Who will function as the enrollment manager? In some ways administrators coming from the ranks of admissions officers seem the most likely candidates to fill this role. In reality this may not be the case.

It is evident that enrollment managers should have public relations skills in addition to good administrative skills. These, however, will not be sufficient. Effective enrollment managers will also have to be comfortable with data analysis and knowledgeable about nonprofit marketing (see Litten's distinction between marketing in profit organizations as opposed to nonprofit organizations, in *Applying Market Research in College Admissions,* 1983, pp. 19–22). They will also need to be comfortable with institutional research techniques and methodologies. Enrollment managers need not be able to actually conduct the research, but they should know the right questions to ask and they should be able to understand the findings that emerge from their questions.

I would suggest that these skills are not always found among admissions officers. In fact, the combination of skills required for the effective management of enrollments is a rare commodity. A major university in the Midwest recently conducted a nationwide search to fill a senior-level administrative position in this field. They had great difficulty finding qualified candidates, and the search process eventually took more than a year.

The enrollment management concept offers the possibility of professionalization of the admissions field, but for many admissions people this will require the acquisition of additional skills and knowledge. The right combination of background and knowledge, however, may be found in areas outside the admissions field. Institutional researchers with administrative experience and human relations skills, faculty members from the disciplines of sociology and psychology, and student affairs professionals with a research and evaluation orientation may be ideal candidates for this emerging area. Two administrators who were among the first to develop the enrollment management concept are John MacGuire, formerly of Boston College in Chestnut Hill, Massachusetts, and Tom Huddleston, of Bradley University in Peoria, Illinois. MacGuire is a physicist by training; Huddleston is the vice-provost for student affairs at Bradley.

The potential for the concept of enrollment management is real. The actual implementation of an enrollment management model depends on the answers to two important questions: First, will enrollment managers be given the kind of authority, responsibility, and resources they will need to do their jobs effectively? Second, will potential enrollment managers develop the competencies required to do the tasks involved in such an approach? The failure to fulfill either of these requirements is likely to result in a poorly implemented enrollment management operation.

## MANAGING ENROLLMENTS?

Although the term *enrollment management* has been used throughout this book, the concept clearly involves a complex set of variables that are difficult to actually control or manage. How does an administrator "manage" college choice or "control" the demand for higher education? Despite all the research and programmatic efforts in retention, many colleges and universities have failed to have a significant impact on their retention rates. The notion of student-institution fit remains somewhat elusive, and we do not yet completely understand how college environments interact with student characteristics to effect changes in students.

Actually, *enrollment influencing* is a more accurate term. Enrollments cannot be managed in the same sense that the office of business and finance manages an institution's cash flow or in the same way the staff of an office is managed. Colleges and universities can, nevertheless, influence their enrollments. An understanding of the college-choice process, the role of financial aid, the implications of retention literature, and the impact and outcomes of higher education, when coupled with nonprofit marketing and a well-organized institutional research effort, *can* influence enrollments. Enrollment influencing can lead to greater institutional health and vitality.

# Bibliography

Adkins, D. L. 1975. *The great American degree machine.* New York: McGraw-Hill Book Company.

Alexander, K., et al. 1978. *Status composition and educational goals: An attempt at clarification.* Washington, D.C.: National Institute of Education (ERIC ED 160-537).

Alexander, K., and Cook, M. 1979. *The motivational relevance of educational plans: Questioning the conventional wisdom.* Washington, D.C.: National Institute of Education (ERIC ED 184-404).

Alfred, R. L. 1974. "A conceptual investigation of student attrition in the comprehensive community college." Paper presented at American Educational Research Association.

*A longitudinal study of high school graduates—New York State, fall 1974.* 1974. Albany, N. Y.: State University of New York.

Andersen, C., ed. 1977. *A fact book on higher education.* Washington, D.C.: American Council on Education.

Anderson, C. A., Bowman, M. J., and Tinto, J. V. 1972. *Where colleges are and who attends.* San Francisco: McGraw-Hill Book Company.

Astin, A. W. 1968. *The college environment.* Washington, D.C.: American Council on Education.

Astin, A. W. 1969. Comment on a student's dilemma: Big fish—little pond or little fish—big pond. *Journal of Counseling Psychology* 16; 20–22.

Astin, A. W. 1971. Two approaches to measuring students' perceptions of their college environment. *Journal of College Student Personnel* 12(3): 169–72.

Astin, A. W. 1976. *Preventing students from dropping out.* San Francisco: Jossey-Bass Publishers.

Astin, A. W. 1977. *Four critical years.* San Francisco: Jossey-Bass Publishers.

Astin, A. W., and Holland, J. L. 1961. The environmental assessment technique: A way to measure college environments. *Journal of Educational Psychology* 52: 308–16.

Augenblick, J., and Hyde, W. 1979. *Patterns of funding, net price and financial need for post-secondary education students: Differences among states, institutional sectors and income groups.* Report F-79. Denver, Colo.: Educational Commissioner of the States (ERIC ED 167-006).

Aulepp, L., and Delworth, U. 1976. *Training manual for an ecosystem model: Assessing and designing campus environments.* Boulder, Colo.: Western Interstate Commission for Higher Education.

Aulepp, L., and Delworth, U. 1978. A team approach to environmental assessment. In J. H. Banning (ed.), *Campus ecology: A perspective for student affairs*. Cincinnati, Ohio: National Association for Student Personnel Administrators.

Bacchetti, R. 1980. Planning aid and aiding plans. In J. B. Henry (ed.), *New directions for institutional research: The impact of student financial aid on institutions*. San Francisco: Jossey-Bass Publishers.

Baird, L. L. 1973. *The graduates: A report on the characteristics and plans of college seniors*. Princeton, N.J.: Educational Testing Service.

Baird, L. L., ed. 1977. *New directions for community colleges: Assessing student academic and social programs*. San Francisco: Jossey-Bass Publishers.

Baird, L. L., Hartnett, R. T., and Associates. 1980. *Understanding student and faculty life*. San Francisco: Jossey-Bass Publishers.

Banning, J. H., ed. 1978. *Campus ecology: A perspective for student affairs*. Cincinnati, Ohio: National Association for Student Personnel Administrators.

Banning, J. H. 1980. The campus ecology manager role. In U. Delworth, G. F. Hanson, and Associates (eds.), *Student services: A handbook for the profession*. San Francisco: Jossey-Bass Publishers.

Banning, J. H., and Kaiser, L. 1974. An ecological perspective and model for campus design. *Personnel and Guidance Journal* 52: 370–75.

Banning, J. H., and McKinley, D. L. 1980. Conceptions of the campus environment. In W. H. Morrill, J. C. Hurst, and E. R. Oetting (eds.), *Dimensions of intervention for student development*. New York: John Wiley & Sons.

Barker, R. G. 1968. *Ecological psychology: Concepts and methods for studying the environment of human behavior*. Stanford, Calif.: Stanford University Press.

Barker, R. G., and Gump, P. V. 1964. *Big school, small school*. Stanford, Calif.: Stanford University Press.

Beal, P. E., and Noel, L. 1980. *What works in student retention?* Boulder, Colo., and Iowa City, Iowa: American Council on Testing and National Center for Educational Management Systems.

Bean, J. P. 1980. Dropouts and turnover: The synthesis and test of a causal model of student attrition. *Research in Higher Education* 12: 155–82.

Bean, J. P. 1983. The application of a model of turnover in work organizations to the student attrition process. *Review of Higher Education* 6: 129–48.

Beaton, A. E. 1975. The influences of education and ability on salary and attitudes. In F. T. Juster (ed.), *Education, income, and human behavior*. New York: McGraw-Hill Book Company.

Becker, G. S., ed. 1971. Optimal investment in human capital. In B. F. Kiker (ed.), *Investment in human capital*. Columbia, S.C.: University of South Carolina Press.

Beezer, R. H. and Hjelm. 1961. *Factors related to college attendance*. Washington, D.C.: U.S. Department of Health, Education, and Welfare.

Berg, I. 1970. *Education and jobs: The great train robbery*. New York: Praegar Publishers.

Berg, I., and Freeman, M. 1977. The American workplace: Illusions and realities. *Change* 9(11): 24–30.

Berne, R. 1980. Net price effects on two-year college attendance decisions. *Journal of Educational Finance* 5: 391–414.

Bird, C. 1975. *The case against college*. New York: David McKay Company.

Bishop, J. 1977. The effect of public policies on the demand for higher education. *Journal of Human Resources* 5(4): 285–307.

Blocher, D. H. 1974. Toward an ecology of student development. *Personnel and Guidance Journal* 52: 360–65.

Blocher, D. H. 1978. Campus learning environments and the ecology of student development. In J. H. Banning (ed.), *Campus ecology: A perspective for student affairs.* Cincinnati, Ohio: National Association for Student Personnel Administrators.

Boldt, W. J., and Stroud, J. B. 1934. Changes in attitudes of College Students. *Journal of Educational Psychology* 25: 611–19.

Bolton, C. D., and Kammeyer, K. C. W. 1967. *The university student: A study of student behavior and values.* New Haven, Conn.: College and University Press Services.

Bowen, Howard. 1977. *Investment in learning: Individual and social value of American higher education.* San Francisco: Jossey-Bass Publishers.

Boyd, J., and Fenske, R. 1976. Financing a college education: Theory vs. reality. *Journal of Student Financial Aid* 6: 11–21.

Boyd, J., Fenske, R., and Maxey, E. J. 1978. Trends in meeting college costs over the past ten years. *Journal of Student Financial Aid* 8: 5–17.

Boyd, V., Magoon, T. M., and Leonard, M. 1982. A small sample intervention approach to attrition-retention in higher education. *Journal of College Student Personnel* 23:390–94.

Breneman, D. 1982. "Comments on W. L. Hansen's paper Economic growth and equal opportunity: Conflicting values or complementary goals in higher education." Paper delivered at National Institute of Education Conference on Education, Productivity, and the National Economy.

Breneman, D. 1983. The coming enrollment crisis. *Change* 15(2): 14–19.

Broome, E. C. 1963. *A historical and critical discussion of college admissions requirements.* New York: College Entrance Examination Board.

Brown, D. 1970. A scheme for measuring the output of higher education. In *The outputs of higher education: Their identification, measurement, and evaluation.* Boulder, Colo.: Western Interstate Commission on Higher Education.

Brown, R. D. 1968. Manipulation of the environmental press in a college residence hall. *Personnel and Guidance Journal* 46(6): 555–60.

Brubacher, J. S., and Rudy, W. 1976. *Higher education in transition: A history of American higher education, 1636–1976.* New York: Harper & Row Publishers.

Budig, J. E., and Sallach, D. 1981. "Student outcomes assessment: A biracial analysis." Paper presented at the Association of Institutional Research (ERIC ED 205–075).

Campbell, R., and Siegel, B. N. 1967. The demand for higher education in the U.S., 1919–1964. *American Economic Review* 21: 483–93.

Carnegie Council on Policy Studies in Higher Education 1979. *The next step for the 1980's in student financial aid: A fourth alternative.* San Francisco: Jossey-Bass Publishers.

Carnegie Council on Policy Studies in Higher Education 1980. *Three thousand futures: The next twenty years for higher education.* San Francisco: Jossey-Bass Publishers.

Carroll, S. J., et al. 1977. *The enrollment effects of federal student aid policies.* Santa Monica, Calif.: Rand Corporation.

Cartter, A. 1966. The supply and demand of college teachers. *Journal of Human Resources* 1: 22–38.

Centra, J. A. 1968. Studies of institutional environments: Categories of instrumentation and some issues. In E. Fincher (ed.), *Institutional research and academic outcomes: Proceedings of the eighth annual forum of the association for institutional research.*

Centra, J. A. 1970. The college environment revisited: Current descriptions and a . comparison of three methods of assessment. *College entrance examination board research and development reports.* RDR-70-71, No. 1. Princeton, N.J.: Educational Testing Service.

Chapman, David 1981. A model of student college choice. *Journal of Higher Education* 52: 490–505.

Chapman, R. G. 1979. Pricing policy and the college choice process. *Research in Higher Education* 10: 37–57.

Chapman, R. G. 1984. *Toward a theory of college choice: A model of college search and choice behavior.* Alberta, Canada: University of Alberta.

Chickering, A. W. 1969. *Education and identity.* San Francisco: Jossey-Bass Publishers.

Chickering, A. W. 1974. *Commuting versus residential students.* San Francisco: Jossey-Bass Publishers.

Chickering, A. W., and Kuper, E. 1971. Educational outcomes for commuters and residents. *Educational Record* 52: 225–61.

*Chronicle of Higher Education.* 1978. 16(5): 8.

*Chronicle of Higher Education.* 1981. 23(10): 1.

*Chronicle of Higher Education.* 1982. 25(13): 2, 7, 9.

Churchill, W. D., and Iwai, S. I. 1981. College attrition, student use of campus facilities, and a consideration of self-reported personal problems. *Research in Higher Education* 14: 105–13.

Clark, B. R., and Trow, M. 1966. The organizational context. In T. M. Newcomb and E. K. Wilson (eds.), *College peer groups: Problems and prospects for research.* Chicago: Aldine Publishing Company.

Coleman, J. S. 1966. Peer culture and education in modern society. In T. M. Newcomb and E. K. Wilson (eds.), *College peer groups: Problems and prospects for research.* Chicago: Aldine Publishing Company.

College Board. 1976. *Making it count: A report on a project to provide better financial aid information to students.* New York: College Entrance Examination Board.

College Board. 1977. *Student aid: Institutional packaging and family expenditure patterns. National longitudinal study of the high school class of 1972.* New York: College Entrance Examination Board.

College Board. 1981. *Student aid and the urban poor.* New York: College Entrance Examination Board.

College Board. 1984. *Enrollment planning service.* New York: College Entrance Examination Board.

Conklin, M. E., and Dailey, A. R. 1981. Does consistency of parental educational encouragement matter for secondary students? *Sociology of Education* 54: 254–62.

Cope, R. G., and Hannah, W. 1975. *Revolving college doors: The causes and consequences of dropping out, stopping out, and transferring.* New York: John Wiley & Sons.

Corrazzini, A. J., Dugan, D. J., and Grabowski, H. G. 1972. Determinants of and distributional aspects of enrollment in U.S. higher education. *Journal of Human Resources* 7: 39–59.

Corwin, T., and Kent, L., eds. 1978. *Tuition and student aid: Their relation to college enrollment decisions.* Washington, D.C.: American Council on Education.

Craft, L. N., and Howard, M. D. 1979. Financial aid: Just a recruiting tool? *Journal of Student Financial Aid* 9: 33–38.

Creager, J. A. 1968. Use of research results in matching students and colleges. *Journal of College Student Personnel* 9: 312–19.

Crossland, F. 1980. Learning to cope with the downward slope. *Change* 12(5): 18–25.

Davis, J. S., and Van Dusen, W. D. 1978. *Guide to the literature of student financial aid.* New York: College Entrance Examination Board.

Deitch, K. 1982. Who qualifies for financial aid? In M. Kramer (ed.), *New directions for higher education: Meeting student aid needs in a period of retrenchment.* San Francisco: Jossey-Bass Publishers.

Dennison, E. F. 1971. Source of past and future growth. In R. Wykstra (ed.), *Human capital formation and manpower development.* New York: The Free Press.

Dickmeyer, Nathan, Wessels, J., and Goldren, S. L. 1981. *Institutionally funded student financial aid.* Washington, D.C.: American Council on Education.

Doerman, H. 1968. *Crosscurrents in college admissions: Institutional response to student ability and family income.* New York: Teachers College Press, Columbia University.

Douglas, G. K. 1977. Economic returns on investments in higher education. In H. Bowen, *Investment in learning: Individual and societal value of American higher education.* San Francisco: Jossey-Bass Publishers.

Dresch, S. P., and Waldenberg, A. L. 1978. *Labor market incentives, intellectual competence and college attendance.* New Haven, Conn.: Institute for Demographic and Economic Studies.

Dressel, P., and Associates. 1971. *Institutional research in the university: A handbook.* San Francisco: Jossey-Bass Publishers.

Eckaus, A. S., El Safty, A., and Norman, V. D. 1974. An appraisal of the calculations of rates of return to higher education. In Margaret S. Gordon (ed.), *Higher education and the labor market.* New York: McGraw-Hill Book Company.

Educational Testing Service. 1972. *The institutional goals inventory.* Princeton, N.J.: Educational Testing Service.

Ekehammer, B. 1974. Interactionism in personality from a historical perspective. *Psychological Bulletin* 81(12): 1026–48.

El-Khawas, E., and Henderson, C. 1982. "A commentary on economic growth and equal opportunity: Conflicting or complementary goals in higher education?" Paper prepared for the Division of Policy Analysis and Research. Washington, D.C.: American Council on Education.

Elliott, W. F. 1980. Financial aid decisions and implications of market management. In J. B. Henry (ed.), *New directions for institutional research: The impact of student financial aid on institutions*. San Francisco: Jossey-Bass Publishers.

Endo, J., and Harpel, R. 1980. "A longitudinal study of student outcomes of a state university." Paper presented at American Institutional Research Forum (ERIC ED 189-927).

Endo, J., & Harpel R. 1981. "The effects of student faculty interaction on student educational outcomes." Paper presented at American Institutional Research Forum (ERIC ED 205-086).

Ewell, P. T. 1983. *Student-outcomes questionnaires: An implementation handbook*. Boulder, Colo.: National Center for Educational Management Systems.

Feldman, K. A., and Newcomb, T. M. 1969. *The impact of college on students,* vols. 1 and 2. San Francisco: Jossey-Bass Publishers.

Feldman, P. and Hoenack, S. 1969. Private demand for higher education in the United States. *The economics and financing of higher education in the United States.* The Joint Economic Committee.

Fenske, R., Boyd, J., and Maxey, E. J. 1979. State financial aid: A trend analysis of access and choice of public and private colleges. *College and University* 54: 137–55.

Fetters, W. B. 1977. *Withdrawal from institutions of higher education: An appraisal with longitudinal data involving diverse institutions*. National Center for Educational Statistics, Washington, D.C.: United States Office of Education.

Frances, Carol. 1980. *College enrollment trends? Testing the conventional wisdom against the facts*. Washington, D.C.: American Council on Education.

Frances, Carol. 1983. 1984: The outlook for higher education. *AAHE Bulletin,* December 3–6.

Freedman, M. B. 1967. *The college experience*. San Francisco: Jossey-Bass Publishers.

Freeman, R. 1971. *The market for college-trained manpower: A study in the economics of career choice*. Cambridge, Mass.: Harvard University Press.

Freeman, R. 1975. Overinvestment in college training. *Journal of Human Resources* 3: 287–311.

Freeman, R. 1976. *The over-educated American*. New York: Academic Press.

Freeman, R. 1980. The facts about the declining economic value of college. *Journal of Human Resources* 15: 124–42.

Freeman, R., and Holloman, J. H. 1975. The declining value of college going. *Change* 7(7): 24–31.

Froomkin, J. 1980. *Education and earnings*. Washington, D.C.: Educational Policy Research Center for Higher Education and Society (ERIC ED 202-273).

Froomkin, J., and Jaffe, A. J. 1978. Occupational opportunities for college-educated workers, 1956–75, *Monthly Labor Review* 3: 14–21.

Gaff, J. 1973. Making a difference: The impact of faculty. *Journal of Higher Education* 8: 605–22.

Galper, H., and Dunn, R. N., Jr. 1969. A short-run demand function for higher education in the U.S. *Journal of Political Economy* 15: 765–77.

Ghali, M., Miklius, W., and Wada, H. 1977. The demand for higher education facing an individual institution. *Higher Education* 6: 477–87.

Gibson, R. J. 1982. New realities for financial aid. In M. Kramer (ed.), *New directions for higher education: Meeting student aid needs in a period of retrenchment.* San Francisco: Jossey-Bass Publishers.

Gillespie, D. A., and Carlson, Nancy. 1983. *Trends in student financial aid: 1963 to 1983.* New York: College Entrance Examination Board.

Glover, S. 1978. The middle-income squeeze. *Journal of Student Financial Aid* 8: 29–34.

Gordon, M. S., ed. 1974. *Higher education and the labor market.* New York: McGraw-Hill Book Company.

Gordon, M. S., and Alhadeff, Carol. 1980. The labor market and higher education. In the Carnegie Council on Policy Studies in Higher Education, *Three thousand futures: The next twenty years for higher education.* San Francisco: Jossey-Bass Publishers.

Gordon, V. 1982. Reasons for entering college and academic and vocational preferences. *Journal of College Student Personnel* 23: 371–77.

Hansen, W. L. 1982. "Economic growth and equal opportunity: Conflicting values or complementary goals in higher education." Paper supported by Institute for Research on Poverty. Madison, Wis.: University of Wisconsin.

Hapgood, D. 1971. *Diplomaism.* New York: Donald W. Brown.

Harnqvist, K. 1978. *Individual demand for higher education: Analytical report.* Paris, France: Organization for Economic Cooperation and Development (ERIC ED 159-119).

Harris, S. 1964. *The economic aspects of higher education.* Paris, France: Organization for Economic Cooperation and Development.

Hauptman, A. 1982. Shaping alternative loan programs. In M. Kramer (ed.), *New directions for higher education: Meeting student aid needs in a period of retrenchment.* San Francisco: Jossey-Bass Publishers.

Hause, J. C. 1969. Ability and schooling as determinants of lifetime earnings; or, if you're so smart why aren't you rich? *American Economic Review* 23: 289–98.

Hauser, J. Z., and Lazarsfeld, P. F. 1964. *The admissions officer in the American college: An occupation under change.* New York: College Entrance Examination Board.

Hearn, J. 1980. Effects on enrollment of changes in student aid policies and programs. In J. B. Henry (ed.), *New directions for institutional research: The impact of student financial aid on institutions.* San Francisco: Jossey-Bass Publishers.

Henry, J. B., ed. 1980. *New directions for institutional research: The impact of student financial aid on institutions.* San Francisco: Jossey-Bass Publishers.

Herndon, S. 1982. The efficacy of student financial aid: Are the proposed funding reductions and program limitations warranted and in the best interest of America's citizenry? *Journal of Student Financial Aid* 12: 37–44.

Hillery, M. C. 1978. Maintaining enrollments through career planning. In L. Noel (ed.), *New directions for student services: Reducing the dropout rate.* San Francisco: Jossey-Bass Publishers.

Hilton, T. L. 1982. *Persistence in higher education.* New York: College Entrance Examination Board.

Hodgkinson, V. 1982. Fifteen ways to stretch scarce student aid. In M. Kramer (ed.), *New directions for higher education: Meeting student aid needs in a period of retrenchment.* San Francisco: Jossey-Bass Publishers.

Hoenack, S. 1971. The efficient allocation of subsidies to college students. *American Economic Review* 61: 302–12.

Holland, J. L. 1971. *The self-directed search.* Palo Alto, Calif.: Consulting Psychologists Press.

Holland, J. L. 1973. *Making vocational choices: A theory of careers.* Englewood Cliffs, N.J.: Prentice-Hall.

Hossler, D. 1979. "College enrollment: The impact of declining pecuniary benefits." Unpublished Ph.D. dissertation, Claremont, Calif.: Claremont Graduate School.

Hossler, D. 1982. College enrollment: The impact of perceived economic benefits. *College and University* 58: 85–96.

Huebner, L. A. 1980. Interaction of student and campus. In U. Delworth, G. R. Hanson, and Associates (eds.), *Student services: A handbook for the profession.* San Francisco: Jossey-Bass Publishers.

Huebner, L. A., and Corrazzini, J. G. 1976. Ecomapping: A dynamic model for interventional campus design. *Student development staff papers* 6. Fort Collins, Colo.: Colorado State University.

Hyde, W., Jr. 1977. "The effect of tuition and financial aid on student choice in postsecondary education." Paper presented at the Postsecondary Educational Finance Conference (ERIC ED 153-541).

Iffert, R. E. 1958. *Retention and withdrawal of college students.* Washington, D.C.: United States Department of Health, Education, and Welfare.

Ihlanfeldt, W. 1980. *Achieving optimal enrollments and tuition revenues.* San Francisco: Jossey-Bass Publishers.

Insel, P. L., and Moos, R. H. 1974. Psychological environments: Expanding the scope of human ecology. *American Psychologist* 29: 179–89.

Iwai, S., and Churchill, W. D. 1982. College attrition and the financial support system of students. *Research in Higher Education* 17: 105–13.

Jackson, Gregory. 1978. Financial aid and student enrollment. *Journal of Higher Education* 49: 548–74.

Jackson, Gregory. 1980. *Efficiency and enrollment modification in higher education, project report No. 80-A-5.* Palo Alto, Calif.: Stanford University Institute for Research on Educational Finance and Governance (ERIC ED 188-328).

Jackson, Gregory. 1982. Public efficiency and private choice in higher education. *Educational Evaluation and Policy Analysis* 4(2): 237–47.

Jackson, Gregory, and Weathersby, G. 1975. Individual demand for higher education. *Journal of Higher Education* 46: 623–52.

Jackson, J., and Levine, D. 1977. Treatment environment and staff ideology in two British mental hospitals. *American Journal of Community Psychology* 5(3): 307–19.

Jedamus, P., Peterson, M., and Associates. 1980. *Improving academic management: A handbook of planning and institutional research.* San Francisco: Jossey-Bass Publishers.

Jencks, C., and Reisman, D. 1968. *The academic revolution.* New York: Doubleday & Company.

Jencks, C. et al. 1977. *Who gets ahead? The determinants of success in America.* New York: Basic Books, Publishers.

Jensen, E. L. 1981. Student financial aid and persistence. *Journal of Higher Education* 52: 280–94.

Jensen, E. L. 1983. Financial aid and educational outcomes: A review. *College and University* 59: 287–302.

Jones, V. 1982. *Report on evaluating educational outcomes: A Nazareth College planning perspective* (ERIC ED 219-024).

Juster, F. T., ed. 1975. *Education, income and human behavior.* New York: McGraw-Hill Book Company.

Kaiser, L. R. 1975. Designing campus environments. *NASPA Journal* 13(1): 33–39.

Kaiser, L. R. 1978. Campus ecology and campus design. In J. H. Banning (ed.), *Campus ecology: A perspective for student affairs.* Cincinnati, Ohio: National Association for Student Personnel Administrators.

Kantor, J. R. 1924. *Principles of psychology,* vol. 1. Bloomington, Ind.: Principia Press.

Keeley, S. M., Browne, M. N., and Kreutzer, J. S. 1982. A comparison of freshmen and seniors on general and specific essay tests of critical thinking. *Research in Education* 17: 139–54.

Kehoe, J. J. 1981. Migrational choice patterns in financial aid policymaking. *Research in Higher Education* 14: 57–69.

Kelly, R. N. 1980. High costs, high need: The independent college and student assistance. In J. B. Henry (ed.), *New directions for institutional research: The impact of student financial aid on institutions.* San Francisco: Jossey-Bass Publishers.

Kemerer, F. R., Baldridge, J. V., and Green, K. C. 1982. *Strategies for effective enrollment management.* Washington, D.C.: American Association of State Colleges and Universities.

Keniston, K. 1966. The faces in the lecture room. In R. S. Morison (ed.), *The contemporary university: U.S.A.* Boston: Houghton Mifflin Company.

Kent, L., and Astin, H. 1983. Gender roles in transition: Research and policy implications for higher education. *Journal of Higher Education* 54: 309–24.

Kiker, B. F., ed. 1971. *Investment in human capital.* Columbia, S.C.: University of South Carolina Press.

Kohn, M. C., Manski, F., and Mundel, D. 1972. "A study of college choice." Paper presented at the North American Regional Meeting of the Econometric Society.

Kolstad, A. 1979. "The influence of high school type and curriculum on enrollment in higher education and post-secondary training." Paper presented at American Educational Research Association Conference.

Kotler, P. 1975. *Marketing for non-profit organizations.* Englewood Cliffs, N.J.: Prentice-Hall.

Kotler, P., and Murphy, P. E. 1981. Strategic planning for higher education. *The Journal of Higher Education* 52(5): 470–89.

Kramer, M., ed. 1982. *New directions for higher education: Meeting student aid needs in a period of retrenchment.* San Francisco: Jossey-Bass Publishers.

Lacy, W. B. 1978. Interpersonal relationships as mediators of structural effects: College student socialization in a traditional and experimental environment. *Sociology of Education* 51: 201–11.

Lamden, L. 1982. Changing through cooperation. *Change* 14(8): 27–29.

Landis, H. L. 1963. Dissonance between student and college variables related to success and satisfaction. *Dissertation Abstracts International* 25(2): 1047–48.

Lauterbach, C. G., and Vielhaber, D. P. 1966. Need-press and expectation-press indices as predictors of college achievement. *Educational and Psychological Measurement* 26: 965–72.

Lawton, M. P. 1977. The impact of environment on aging. In J. E. Birren and K. W. (eds.), *Handbook on the psychology of aging.* New York: Van Nostrand Reinhold.

Leibowitz, A. 1975. Education and allocation of women's time. In F. T. Juster (ed.), *Education, income and human behavior.* New York: McGraw-Hill Book Company.

Lenning, O. T., and Beal, P. E., eds. 1976. *New directions for higher education: Improving educational outcomes.* San Francisco: Jossey-Bass Publishers.

Lenning, O. T., Sauer, K., and Beal, P. E. 1980a. *Student retention strategies.* AAHE-ERIC/Higher Education Research Report no. 8. Washington, D.C.: American Association for Higher Education.

Lenning, O. T., Sauer, K., and Beal, P. E. 1980b. *Retention and attrition: Evidence for action and research.* Boulder, Colo.: National Center for Higher Education Management Systems.

Levine, A. 1980. *When dreams and heroes died: A portrait of today's college student.* San Francisco: Jossey-Bass Publishers.

Lewin, K. 1936. *Principles of topological psychology.* New York: McGraw-Hill Book Company.

Lewis, C., Leach, E., and Lutz, L. 1983. A marketing model for student retention. *NASPA Journal* 20(3): 15–24.

Linney, T. 1979. Interstate migration of college students. *AAHE-ERIC/Higher Education Research Currents.* December 1979.

Litten, L. H. 1982. Different strokes in the applicant pool: Some refinements in a model of student choice. *Journal of Higher Education* 4: 383–402.

Litten, L. H., Sullivan, Daniel, and Brodigan, D. L. 1983. *Applying market research in college admissions.* New York: College Entrance Examination Board.

Lopatin, A. 1984. Student reactions to college recruiting. In College Board, *Admissions Strategist.* New York: College Entrance Examination Board.

Lowery, W. R., and Associates. 1982. *College admissions counseling.* San Francisco: Jossey-Bass Publishers.

McClelland, D. C., et al. 1958. *Talent and society: New perspectives in the identification of talent.* New York: D. Van Nostrand Company.

McConnell, W. R., and Kaufman, N. 1984. *High school graduates: Projections for the fifty states.* Boulder, Colo.: Western Interstate Commission on Higher Education.

McCreight, K., and LeMay, M. 1982. A longitudinal study of the achievement and persistence of students who receive basic opportunity grants. *Journal of Student Financial Aid* 12: 11–15.

McCuen, J. T. Colleges incredibly effective in fighting unemployment. *Community and Junior College Journal* 53: 20–21.

McDowell, J. V., and Chickering, A. W. 1976. *The experience of college questionnaire.* Plainfield, Vt.: Project on Student Development.

McLaughlin, G., Mahon, B. T., and Montgomery, J. 1981. "Alumni perceptions: A test of NCHEM's outcomes structure." Paper presented at Association of Institutional Research Forum (ERIC ED 205-069).

McQuitty, J. V., and Tully, G. E. 1969. *Plans beyond high school: A report of a survey of statewide Florida high school seniors, Fall, 1969.* Tallahassee, Fla.: Florida State Board of Regents.

Machlup, F. 1970. *Education and economic growth.* Lincoln, Nebr.: University of Nebraska.

Maguire, J., and Lay, R. 1980. Identifying the competition in higher education. *College and University* 56: 53–65.

Maguire, J., and Lay, R. 1981. Modeling the college choice process. *College and University* 56(2): 123–39.

Manski, C. F., and Wise, D. A. 1983. *College choice in America.* Cambridge, Mass.: Harvard University Press.

Mare, R. D. 1979. Social background composition and educational growth. *Demography* 16: 55–71.

Mattila, J. P. 1982. Determinants of male school enrollments: A time series analysis. *Review of Economics and Statistics* 64: 242–51.

Mauss, A. L. 1967. "Toward an empirical typology of junior college student subcultures." Paper presented at the Pacific Sociological Association.

Michigan Consortium for the Evaluation of Nontraditional Education. 1981. *Experiential learning programs and liberal studies.* Mt. Pleasant: Michigan Consortium for the Evaluation of Nontraditional Learning Programs (ERIC ED 202-436).

Miller, L. S. 1976. *Demand and supply in U.S. higher education: A technical supplement.* (ERIC ED 116-584).

Moos, R. H. 1973. Conceptualizations of human environments. *American Psychologist* 28: 652–65.

Moos, R. H. 1974. Systems for the assessment and classifications of human environments: An overview. In R. H. Moos and P. Insel (eds.), *Issues in Social Ecology.* Palo Alto, Calif.: National Press Books.

Moos, R. H. 1976a. *Community-oriented programs scale manual.* Palo Alto, Calif.: Consulting Psychologists Press.

Moos, R. H. 1976b. *Correctional institutions environment scale manual.* Palo Alto, Calif.: Consulting Psychologists Press.

Moos, R. H. 1976c. *Family environment scale manual.* Palo Alto, Calif.: Consulting Psychologists Press.

Moos, R. H. 1976d. *The human context: Environmental determinants of behavior.* New York: Wiley-Interscience.

Moos, R. H. 1976e. *Ward atmosphere scale manual.* Palo Alto, Calif.: Consulting Psychologists Press.

Moos, R. H. 1979. *Evaluating educational environments.* San Francisco: Jossey-Bass Publishers.

Moos, R. H., and Gerst, M. 1976. *University residence environment scale manual.* Palo Alto, Calif.: Consulting Psychologists Press.

Moos, R. H., and Humphrey, B. 1976. *Group environment scale manual.* Palo Alto, Calif.: Consulting Psychologists Press.

Moos, R. H., and Insel, R. 1976. *Work environment scale manual.* Palo Alto, Calif.: Consulting Psychologists Press.

Moos, R. H., and Trickett, E. 1976. *Classroom environment scale manual.* Palo Alto, Calif.: Consulting Psychologists Press.

Morrill, W. H. 1973. "Institutional assessment and counseling outreach." Grant application to Department of Health, Education, and Welfare, Public Health Service.

Morrow, J. M., Jr. 1971. A test of Holland's theory of vocational choice. *Journal of Counseling Psychology* 18: 422–25.

Murray, H. A. 1938. *Explorations in personality.* New York: Oxford University Press.

Muston, R. 1984. Enrollment strategies among selected state universities. Paper delivered at the Annual Meeting of the Association for the Study of Higher Education, Chicago.

Nafziger, D. H., Holland, J. L., and Gottfredron, G. D. 1975. Student-college congruency as a predictor of satisfaction. *Journal of Counseling Psychology* 22(2): 132–39.

National Commission on Financing Postsecondary Education. 1973. *Financing postsecondary education in the United States.* Washington, D.C.: U.S. Government Printing Office.

Naylor, P., and Sanford, T. (1980). "Educational maturity, race and the selection of college." A paper presented at the Association for Institutional Research Forum (ERIC ED 189-954).

Nelson, J. E. 1984. The College Board: Interoffice memorandum, March 5.

Newlon, L., and Gaither, G. 1980. Factors Contributing to Attrition: An Analysis of Program Impact on Persistence Patterns. *College and University* 55: 237–51.

Noel, L., ed. 1978. *New directions for student services: Reducing the dropout rate.* San Francisco: Jossey-Bass Publishers.

Olivas, M. 1981. *Financial aid: Access and packaging policies for disadvantaged students.* Institute for Research on Educational Finance and Governance. Program Report no. 81-B14. Palo Alto, Calif.: Stanford University.

Open University. 1978. *Planning of higher education: The private demand, a third-level course, economics and educational policy I.* Walton, Blechtley, England: Open University, P.O. Box 4B (ERIC ED 181-842).

Ott, L. 1978. Admissions and retention. In L. Noel (ed.), *New directions for student services: Reducing the dropout rate.* San Francisco: Jossey-Bass Publishers.

Pace, C. R. 1958. An approach to the measurement of psychosocial characteristics of college environment. *Journal of Educational Psychology* 49(5): 269–77.

Pace, C. R. 1969. *College and university environment scales technical manual,* 2d. ed. Princeton, N.J.: Educational Testing Service.

Pace, C. R. 1972. *Education and evangelism: A profile of Protestant colleges.* New York: McGraw-Hill Book Company

Pace, C. R. 1979. *Measuring the outcomes of college: Fifty years of findings and recommendations for the future.* San Francisco: Jossey-Bass Publishers.

Pace, C. R. 1980. Assessing diversity among campus groups. In L. L. Baird, R. T. Hartnett, and Associates (eds.), *Understanding student and faculty life*. San Francisco: Jossey-Bass Publishers.

Pace, C. R., and Stern, G. G. 1958. An approach to the measurement of psychological characteristics of college environments. *Journal of Educational Psychology* 49(5): 269–77.

Packer, J. 1980. Student aid and student need on campus. In J. B. Henry (ed.), *New directions for institutional research: The impact of student aid on institutions*. San Francisco: Jossey-Bass Publishers.

Painter, P., and Painter, N. 1982. Placing students for stability and success. In W. R. Lowery and Associates (eds.), *College admissions counseling*. San Francisco: Jossey-Bass Publishers.

Pantages, T. J., and Creedon, C. 1968. Attrition among college students. *American Educational Research Journal* 5: 57–72.

Pascarella, E. T., and Terenzini, P. T. 1980a. Patterns of student-faculty interaction beyond the classroom and voluntary freshman attrition. *Journal of Higher Education* 48: 540–52.

Pascarella, E. T., and Terenzini, P. T. 1980b. Predicting freshman persistence and voluntary dropout decisions from a theoretical model. *Journal of Higher Education* 51: 60–75.

Pascarella, E. T., Duby, P., Miller, V., and Rasher, S. 1981. Preenrollment variables and academic performance as predictors of freshman year persistence, early withdrawal, and stopout behavior in an urban, nonresidential university. *Research in Higher Education* 15: 329–49.

Pascarella, E. T., and Chapman, D. 1983. A multiinstitutional path analytic validation of Tinto's model of withdrawal. *American Educational Research Journal* 20: 111–24.

Pascharopoulus, G. 1975. *Earnings and education in OECD countries*. Paris: Organization for Economic Development.

Pemberton, W. A. 1963. *Ability, values, and college achievement*. University of Delaware Studies in Higher Education, no. 1. Newark: University of Delaware.

Pepin, W. B. and Korb, R. A. 1979. "A study of non-cognitive and cognitive characteristics as predictors of high school seniors' early post-secondary activities." Paper presented at American Educational Research Foundation.

Perlman, R. 1973. *The economics of higher education: Conceptual problems and policy issues*. New York: McGraw-Hill Book Company.

Pervin, L. A. 1967. A twenty-college study of student-college interaction using TAPE (transactional analysis of personality and environment): Rationale, reliability, and validity. *Journal of Educational Psychology* 58: 290–302.

Pervin, L. A. 1968. Performance and satisfaction as a function of individual environment fit. *Psychological Bulletin* 69: 56–58.

Peters, W. B. 1977. *Fulfillment of short-term educational plans and continuance in education. National longitudinal study of high school seniors*. Washington, D.C.: National Center for Educational Statistics.

Peterson, R. E. 1968. *Technical manual: College student questionnaire*, ref. ed. Princeton, N.J.: Educational Testing Service.

Peterson, R. E., and Smith C. 1979. *Migration of college students: Preliminary analysis of trend in college student migration.* Washington D.C.: Department of Health, Education, and Welfare (ERIC ED 167-038).

Prather, J. E., and Sturgeon, J. E. 1981. "Where will the financial aid ax fall? An empirical model of the impact." Paper presented at the Association for Institutional Research.

Proceedings of the Annual Convention of the Middle States Association of Colleges. 1979. *Outcomes assessment: A new era in accreditation* (ERIC ED 222-102).

Radner, Roy, and Miller, L. S. 1970. Demand and supply in higher education: A progress report. *American Economic Review* 60: 327–34.

Radner, Roy, and Miller, L. S. 1975. *Demand and supply in U.S. higher education.* New York: McGraw-Hill Book Company.

Ramist, Leonard. 1981. *College student attrition and retention.* College Board Report no. 81-1. New York: College Entrance Examination Board.

Rawlins, L., and Ulman, L. 1975. The utilization of college-trained manpower in the U.S. In M. S. Gordon (ed.), *Higher education and the labor market.* New York: McGraw-Hill Book Company.

Reisman, D. 1980. *On higher education. The academic enterprise in an era of rising consumerism.* San Francisco: Jossey-Bass Publishers.

Reitzes, D. C., and Mutran, E. 1980. Significant others and self-conceptions: Factors influencing educational expectations and academic performance. *Sociology of Education* 53: 21–32.

Rootman, I. 1972. Voluntary withdrawal from a total adult socializing organization: A model. *Sociology of Education* 45: 258–70.

Rosenzweig, R. M. 1982. *Research universities and their patrons.* Berkeley, Calif.: University of California Press.

Rowse, G. 1979. *College enrollments and student access in New York State: Prospects for the 1980's.* Albany: New York State Board of Higher Education (ERIC ED 184-479).

Rowse, G., and Wing, P. 1982. Assessing competitive structures in higher education. *Journal of Higher Education* 53: 656–83.

Rudolph, F. 1962. *The American college and university: A history.* New York: Vintage Books.

Rumberger, R. W. 1982. Recent high school and college experiences of youth: Variations by sex, race, and social class. *Youth and Society* 13: 449–70.

Russell, C. N. 1980. *Survey of grade 12 students' post-secondary plans and aspirations.* Manitoba, Canada: Department of Education, September 1980 (ERIC ED 201-225).

Sanford, N., ed. 1962. *The American college: A psychological and social interpretation of higher learning.* New York: John Wiley & Sons.

Sanford, N. 1967. *Where colleges fail.* San Francisco: Jossey-Bass Publishers.

Schomberg, S., Hendel, D. D., and Bassett, C. L. 1981. "Using the college outcome measurement project to measure college outcomes." Paper read at the Association for Institutional Research Forum (ERIC ED 205-121).

*School enrollments—Social and economic characteristics of students, October 1974.* 1975. Washington, D.C.: U.S. Department of Commerce.

Schultz, T. W. 1963. *The economic value of education.* New York: Columbia University Press.

Schumer, H., and Stanfield, R. 1966. "Assessment of student role orientations in college." Paper read at the American Psychological Association.

Schuster, J., and Coil, A. 1982. The effects of type of college on students. In W. R. Lowery and Associates, *College Admissions Counseling.* San Francisco: Jossey-Bass Publishers.

Sewell, W. H., and Shah, V. P. 1978. Social class, parental encouragement, and educational aspirations. *American Journal of Sociology* 73: 559–72.

Smith, J. P., and Welch, F. 1978. *The overeducated American? A review article.* Santa Monica, Calif.: The Rand Corporation.

Solmon, L. C., and Taubman, P. J. 1973. *Does college matter?* New York: Academic Press.

Solmon, L. C., and Oschner, N. 1978. *New findings on the effects of college.* Washington, D.C.: American Association of Higher Education.

Soper, E. L. 1971. *A study of the factors influencing the post-secondary educational and vocational decisions of Utah high school students.* Washington, D.C.: National Center for Educational Research and Development.

Spady, W. G. 1967. Educational mobility access: Growth and paradoxes. *American Journal of Sociology* 14: 273–286.

Spady, W. G. 1970. Dropouts from higher education: An interdisciplinary review and synthesis. *Interchange* 1: 64–85.

Spady, W. G. 1972. Dropouts from higher education. *Interchange* 2: 38–62.

Spaeth, J., and Greely, A. 1970. *Recent college alumni in higher education.* New York: McGraw-Hill Book Company.

Spies, R. 1973. *The future of private colleges: The effect of rising costs on college choice.* Princeton, N.J.: Industrial Relations Section, Department of Economics, Princeton University.

Spies, R. 1978. *The effect of rising costs on college choice. A study of the application decisions of high ability students.* New York: College Entrance Examination Board (ERIC ED 154-686).

St. John, E., and Byce, C. 1982. The changing federal role in student financial aid. In M. Kramer (ed.), *New directions for higher education: Meeting student aid needs in a period of retrenchment.* San Francisco: Jossey-Bass Publishers.

St. John, E., and Sepenik, R. 1982. A framework for improving the management of financial aid offices. In M. Kramer (ed.), *New directions for higher education: Meeting student aid needs in a period of retrenchment.* San Francisco: Jossey-Bass Publishers.

Stampen, J. 1968. *Conflict, accountability and the Wisconsin idea: Relationships between government and higher education.* Unpublished report (ERIC ED 184-432).

Stampen, J. 1980. *Enrollment trends and college costs.* Prepared for the American Association of State Colleges and Universities (ERIC ED 183-088).

Starr, A., Betz, E. L., and Menne, J. 1972. Differences in college student satisfaction: Academic dropouts, nonacademic dropouts, and nondropouts. *Journal of Counseling Psychology* 19: 318–22.

Stern, G. G. 1964. B = f (P,E). *Journal of Personality Assessment* 28(2): 161–68.

Stern, G. G. 1965. Myth and reality in the American college. *American Association of University Professors Bulletin* 52: 408–11.

Stern, G. G. 1970. *People in context: Measuring person-environment congruence in education and industry.* New York: John Wiley & Sons.

Summerskill, J. 1962. Dropouts from college. In N. Sanford (ed.), *The American college student.* New York: John Wiley & Sons.

Taubman, P., and Wales, T. 1973. Higher education, mental ability and screening. *Journal of Political Economy* 1: 28–55.

Terenzini, P. T., and Pascarella, E. T. 1977. Voluntary freshman attrition and patterns of social and academic integration in a university: A test of a conceptual model. *Research in Higher Education* 6: 25–43.

Terenzini, P. T., and Pascarella, E. T. 1978. The relation of students' precollege characteristics and freshman year experience to voluntary attrition. *Research in Higher Education* 9: 347–66.

Terenzini, P. T., and Pascarella, E. T. 1980. Toward the validation of Tinto's model of college student attrition: A review of recent studies. *Research in Higher Education* 12: 271–82.

Terenzini, P. T., Lorang, W., and Pascarella, E. T. 1981. Predicting freshman persistence and voluntary dropout decisions: A replication. *Research in Higher Education* 15: 109–27.

Terenzini, P. T., and Pascarella, E. T. 1984. Freshman attrition and the residential context. *Review of Higher Education* 7. 111 24.

Thistlewaite, D. L., and Wheeler, N. 1966. Effects of teacher and peer subculture upon student aspirations. *Journal of Educational Psychology* 57: 45–47.

Thresher, B. A. 1966. *College Admissions and the Public Interest.* New York: College Entrance Examination Board.

Thurow, C. L. 1974. Measuring the economic benefits of higher education. In M. S. Gordon (ed.), *Higher education and the labor market.* New York: McGraw-Hill Book Company.

Tierney, M. 1980a. "Student college choice sets: Toward an empirical characterization." Paper presented at the Association for the Study of Higher Education.

Tierney, M. 1980b. The impact of financial aid on student demand for public/private higher education. *Journal of Higher Education* 51: 527–45.

Tillery, D. 1973. *Distribution and differentiation of youth: A study of transition from school to college.* Cambridge, Mass.: Ballinger Publishing Company.

Tillery, D., and Kildegaard, T. 1973. *Educational goals: Attitudes and goals—a comparative study of high school seniors.* Cambridge, Mass.: Ballinger Publishing Company.

Tinto, J. V. 1975. Dropout from higher education: A theoretical synthesis of recent research. *Journal of Educational Research* 45: 89–125.

Trent, J. 1970. *The decision to go to college: An accumulative multivariate process.* Washington, D.C.: Office of Education.

Trent, J., and Medsker, L. 1968. *Beyond high school: A psychological study of 10,000 high school graduates.* San Francisco: Jossey-Bass Publishers.

Valiga, M. J. 1981. "The perceived outcomes of higher education." Paper presented at the Association for Institutional Research (ERIC ED 205-107).

Valiga, M. J. 1982. "Structuring the perceived outcomes of higher education." Paper presented at the Association for Institutional Research (ERIC ED 220-024).

Van Alstyne, C. 1979. *Is there or isn't there a middle income crunch?* Washington, D.C.: American Council on Education (ERIC ED 167-005).

Walsh, W. B. 1973. *Theories of person-environment interaction: Implications for the college student.* Iowa City: The American College Testing Program.

Walsh, W. B. 1975. Some theories of person-environment interaction. *Journal of College Student Personnel* 16(2): 107–13.

Walsh, W. B. 1978. Person-environment interaction. In J. H. Banning (ed.), *Campus ecology: A perspective for student affairs.* Columbus, Ohio: National Association of Student Personnel Administrators.

Walsh, W. B., and Russell, J. H., III. 1969. College major choice and personal adjustment. *Personnel and Guidance Journal* 47(7): 685–88.

Warren, J. R. 1968. Student perceptions of college sub-cultures. *American Educational Research Journal* 5: 213–32.

Weinberg, I. 1978. *Financing higher education in the 80's and beyond* (ERIC ED 168-395).

Werts, C. E., and Whatley, D. J. 1969. A student's dilemma: Big fish—little pond or little fish—big pond. *Journal of Counseling Psychology* 16: 14–19.

Whithey, S. B. 1971. *A degree and what else? Correlates and consequences of a college education.* New York: McGraw-Hill Book Company.

Willingham, W. W. 1970. *Free access higher education.* New York: College Entrance Examination Board.

Willingham, W. W., and Breland, H. M. 1982. *Personal qualities and college admissions.* New York: College Entrance Examination Board.

Wilson, R. C., and Gaff, J. G. 1975. *College professors and their impact on students.* New York: John Wiley & Sons.

Wing, Paul. 1980. Forecasting economic and demographic conditions. In P. Jedamus, M. Peterson, and Associates (eds.), *Improving academic management: A handbook of planning and institutional research.* San Francisco: Jossey-Bass Publishers.

Winter, D., McClelland, D. C., and Stewart, A. 1981. *A new case for the liberal arts.* San Francisco: Jossey-Bass Publishers.

Wykstra, R. A., ed. 1971. *Human capital formation and manpower development.* New York: The Free Press.

Yankelovich, D. 1972. *The changing values on campus.* New York: The Free Press.

Young, A. M. 1982. Labor force patterns of students, graduates, and dropouts, 1981. *Monthly Labor Review* 103(9): 40.

Zemsky, Robert, and Oedel, Penney. 1983. *The structure of college choice.* New York: College Entrance Examination Board.

Zucker J. D., and Nazari-Robati, A. 1982. Tuition and the open door: A relative perspective. *Community/Junior College Quarterly* 6: 145–55.